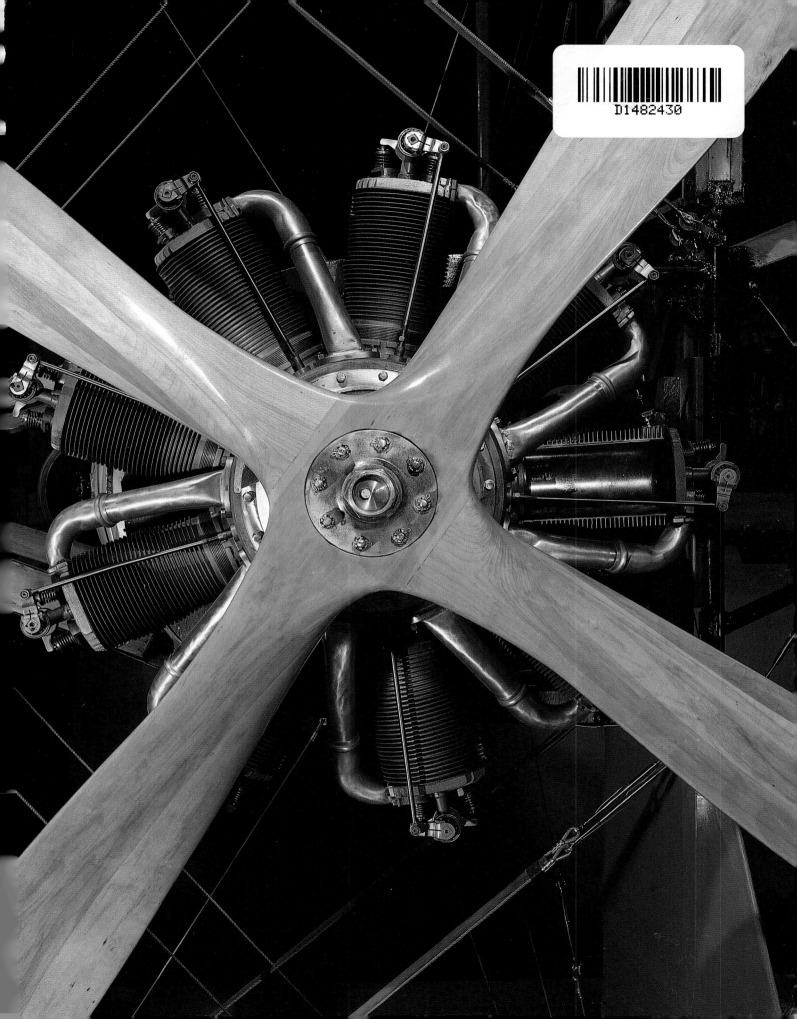

Legend,

Memory
and the
Great War
in the
Air

Dominick A. Pisano

Thomas J. Dietz

Joanne M. Gernstein

Karl S. Schneide

Published for the
National Air and Space Museum, Smithsonian Institution
Washington, D.C.

by the
University of Washington Press
Seattle and London

University of Washington Press
P.O. Box 50096
Seattle, Washington 98145-5096

Library of Congress Cataloging-in-Publication Data

Legend, Memory, and the Great War in the Air / Dominick A. Pisano... [et al.].
        p.   cm.
    Includes bibliographical references and index.
    ISBN 0-295-97215-7 (cloth)   ISBN 0-295-97216-5 (pbk.)

        1. World War, 1914-1918—Aerial operations. 1. Pisano, Dominick.
1943- .   II. National Air and Space Museum.
D600.L44 1992   92-24189
940.4'4—dc20   CIP

The paper used in this publication meets the minimum requirements of American
National Standard for Information Sciences—Permanence of Paper for Printed Materials,
ANSI Z39.48-1984.

Legend, Memory and the Great War in the Air
was produced for the NATIONAL AIR AND SPACE MUSEUM
and the UNIVERSITY OF WASHINGTON PRESS
by PERPETUA PRESS, Los Angeles.
Edited by LETITIA BURNS O'CONNOR
Designed by DANA LEVY
Typeset in Gill Sans and Bookman on a Macintosh II using Pagemaker 4.2
Color separations and filmwork by GOODY COLOR SEP, Hong Kong
Printed and bound by C+C OFFSET PRINTING CO., Hong Kong

CONTENTS

PREFACE

PAUL KENNEDY points out in *The Rise and Fall of the Great Powers: Economic Change and Military Conflict from 1500 to 2000*, that World War I "had been an exhausting struggle for all the original belligerents. Austria-Hungary was gone, Russia in revolution, Germany defeated; yet France, Italy, and even Britain itself had also suffered heavily in their victory. The only exceptions were Japan, which further augmented its position in the Pacific and, of course, the United States, which by 1918 was indisputably the strongest Power in the world." More important than the immediate effects of which Kennedy speaks, however, were the war's long-term effects: the upheaval in the world's social and political order and the transformation of warfare by technology and industry.

One important weapon in World War I was the airplane, which played a significant if not determining role, captured the imagination of the public, and demonstrated its potential for the future. While we may not be aware of it, many of our current beliefs regarding the use of aerial weapons derive from World War I. The memory of the terror inspired by small-scale German bombing raids on civilian targets in England from 1915 to the end of the war helped to shape strategic planning during the years between the wars. Air power was only one of the lessons of the first great war in the air, which, correctly or incorrectly understood, helped to shape the subsequent history of the twentieth century.

Legend, Memory and the Great War in the Air, which opened at the National Air and Space Museum in November 1991, represents a distinct departure from more traditional presentations of the subject. While it discusses the development of aerial strategy and aircraft production, at the deepest level, the exhibition is about history—about the way in which we perceive past events and apply those perceptions in reaching decisions about the future. It provides an accurate portrayal of aviation's role in the war, contrasting the romantic image of gallant combat in the sky with the grim reality faced by the aviators who fought and died in the conflict.

I believe that the principal task of an historical exhibition is to help a museum visitor understand the impact of key events on everyday life—how past experience has shaped today's world. The staff members who worked so hard to produce and mount Legend, Memory and the Great War in the Air have achieved that goal not only in the exhibition itself but also in this book, which addresses the major themes of the show through illuminating narrative, photographs, and documentary materials.

MARTIN HARWIT
Director
National Air and Space Museum

Acknowledgments

THE AUTHORS wish to acknowledge the generous assistance of numerous individuals who made significant contributions to the preparation of the exhibition *Legend, Memory and the Great War in the Air* and to the publication of this book.

Louis Gallois, Chairman and CEO, SNECMA; Jean Bilien, Chairman and CEO, CFMI; Michel Harvey, Managing Director, SNECMA, Ltd.; Jacques Riboni, Executive Vice President, SNECMA, Inc.; Ray Warner, Senior Vice President, DGA International; Erik Jan Nederkoorn, Chairman, Board of Management, Fokker Aircraft, BV; Reinder J. van Duinen, Vice Chairman, Board of Management, Fokker Aircraft, BV; and Stuart Matthews, President and CEO, Fokker Aircraft, USA, were all instrumental in furnishing generous backing for the exhibition.

Tom Freudenheim, Assistant Secretary for Museums, Smithsonian Institution, and his assistant Barbara Schneider supported the exhibition through the Smithsonian Exhibition Fund, which provided two key grants. The family of George Vaughan, Jr., an American ace and member of the U.S. Army Air Service, AEF, who flew with the Royal Air Force, made possible the publication of the brochure that accompanies the exhibition. The Smithson Society of the Smithsonian Institution contributed a grant for the construction of aircraft models.

Our undying gratitude goes to Tom Crouch, Chairman, Aeronautics Department, National Air and Space Museum, who provided an atmosphere in which the curatorial team's creative energy could be given free rein; Terezia Takacs, who designed the exhibition, John Clendening, who assisted her, Frank Florentine, lighting designer, Victor Govier, who served as project coordinator, Patti Woodside, who produced the audiovisuals, David Romanowski, who edited the label script, and Livia Fussi, who designed the advertising poster.

Special thanks to Peter Grosz, Richard Hallion, the late James Hudson, Lee Kennett, John Morrow, Neal O'Connor, Leo Opdycke, Cole Palen, and Steve Woolford, Imperial War Museum, for their consultative expertise and assistance, and to Ted Hamady, Ben Kristy, Guillaume de Syon, and Lisa Wolff for the hours they devotedly volunteered to the project.

Many others participated at various stages of the project. From the National Air and Space Museum, special thanks go to Lin Ezell, Assistant Director for Collections Management, and her staff, including Al Bachmeier, John Eckstine, George Genotti, Richard Horigan, Karl Heinzel, Will Lee, Anne McCombs, Ed McManus, John Liebel, Bob McLean, Matt Nazzaro, Charles Parmley, Bill Reese, Bill Stevenson, Bob Taylor, and Lillie Wiggins, Paul E. Garber Preservation, Restoration and Storage Facility; Ellen Folkama and Natalie Rjedkin, Office of the Registrar; Allan

Janus, Melissa Keiser, Paul Silberman, and Mark Taylor, Archives.

Special thanks go to Nadya Makovenyi, Assistant Director for Exhibits, and her staff, including Sandy Rittenhouse-Black, Derek Fiedler, Dittmar Geiger, Danny Fletcher, Rhawn Anderson, Donald Crowder, Robert Curran, Gary Fletcher, David Gant, Robert Hall, Dave Heck, Richard Hockensmith, Hollis Houston, Eugene Jones, Raymond Jones, Mike Lowry, James Murphy, Gary Newgent, Joan Nicholson, Kena O'Connor, Rich Pullman, Ken Smith, Jefferson Spears, and Norm Taylor.

Others who deserve acknowledgment are Carolyn Schmidt, Office of Education; Bobbie Faul-Zeitler, Joyce Dall'Aqua-Peterson, Patricia Graboske, and Sandy Zafren, Communications Department; Helen McMahon and Jenny Gould, Cooperative Programs; John Carlin, Assistant Director for Development, and his staff including Susan Beaudette, Darlene Rose-Barge, and Jack Van Ness.

Our gratitude also to Peter Jakab, Anita Mason, and Howard Wolko, Aeronautics Department; Don Lopez, Senior Advisor; and Annette Newman, Office of Computer Services.

From the Smithsonian Institution, special thanks go to Ben Snouffer, Jim Reuter, John Siske, Laura Collins, Dick Kilday, Reed Martin, and Tim Smith, Office of Exhibits Central; Mark Avino and Carolyn Russo, Office of Photographic Services; Don Kloster, Ed Ezell, and Harry Hunter, Department of Armed Forces History, National Museum of American History.

From outside the Smithsonian Institution, special thanks go to Elena Millie, Library of Congress; Richard Uppstrom and Jack Hilliard, Air Force Museum; the late Hal Potter, Twentieth Century Fox Movietone News; Douglas Fairbanks, Jr., Stéphan Nicalaou, Valmai and Tony Holt, Nancy Nicolelis, Brad King, Lucien Robineau, Claudia Oakes, Frank Moliter, Douglas H. Robinson, William D. Barr, Richard Keller, and Armando Framarini, U.S. Army Ordnance Museum.

Constructing the Memory of Aerial Combat in World War I

Dominick A. Pisano

"War has nothing to do with chivalry any more...the higher civilization rises, the viler man becomes."[1]

THE MEMORY OF WORLD WAR I WAS reconstructed as a "sacred experience," argues George L. Mosse in *Fallen Soldiers: Reshaping the Memory of the World Wars*. The image makers, Mosse contends, constructed a myth about the war that gave it a religious form and feeling, made saints of the war dead and shrines of their graves, and a provided a heritage that would be carried forward in wars to come. This myth, Mosse asserts, "would draw the sting from death in war and emphasize the meaningfulness of the fighting and sacrifice." The myth served to make acceptable what was intrinsically unacceptable, console the population, and assure the nation that the war had not been fought in vain. More insidious, but no less misleading was the trivialization of the experience of war "through its association with objects of daily life, popular theater, or battlefield tourism."[2]

The pattern of distorting the reality of the war experience in the popular memory and record, which Mosse documents, can also be seen in the history of aviation in the Great War, especially in the minds of the American public. With the passage of time, American perceptions of the air war in World War I have become increasingly skewed, romanticized, and trivialized beyond recognition through the popular culture. The primal reality of World War I was the conflict that took place on the ground—the interminable, bloody, stalemated battles; the estimated eleven million dead; the introduction of new and terrifying weapons; and the inability of leaders to put an end to the slaughter. Yet, what is often remembered best are the heroic struggles of the pilots who fought above the carnage. These efforts, although heroic, have been exaggerated out of all proportion to their importance in the total war.

Academic historians are still perpetuating the old legends. A recent account of the United States' experience in World War I by the American military historian Edward M. Coffman, for example, includes the statement: "the romance and the horror was in the skies of France where it was man against man, a personal war. But before American men and planes could make their mark in combat, great problems in production, training, and administration had to be overcome." Contrary to popular belief, air fighting was not a "personal war," but a difficult and demanding task that required teamwork and offered small margin for error. American men and planes did not effectively "make their mark in combat," repeating the same mistakes as the other combatants, and the problems in production, training, and administration were never overcome.[3]

Why is the history of air combat in World War I so distorted and detached from the reality of the combat on the ground? The answer is two-part. First, historical accounts have too often emphasized the fantasy and adventure that are the intrinsic elements of aerial combat in World War I, rather than chronicling the subject with cold-blooded analysis. Second, the public memory of an historical event is often shaped by misconceptions. Since the writing of history and the process of memory are centrally connected, historians and the public must find ways to integrate the two.

In *Memory and American History*, David Thelen proposes two processes by which memory transforms historical reality. First, Thelen says, "memory, private and individual as much as collective and cultural, is constructed, not reproduced." Second, the construction of memory "is not made in isolation, but in conversations with others that occur in the contexts of community, broader politics, and social dynamics."[4]

During the years that have elapsed since the Great War was fought, two distinct constructions have shaped the memory of the air war. The first is the lionization of the fighter aces, those intrepid "knights of the air" whose exploits have come to define aviation in World War I. The veneration of the fighter pilots is the result of information trivialized through popular culture, especially popular books, magazines, and films. The second, more important construction of the memory of aerial warfare in the Great War is what was appropriated from it to make the case for strategic bombing. This construction provided the framework for the planning and implementation of air power during World War II and continues to influence judgment in the 1990s.

World War I Aviation and the Popular Culture

How did popular culture so influence the memory of World War I aviation? Experts have long recognized the importance of mass media in defining American values. In psychological terms, the public is gratified by and identifies with a hero, transfers this identification to fictional heros, who along with their rank, attributes, and features, become important transmitters of social values.[5]

The legend of aviation in World War I matured during the 1930s, which was, not coincidentally, the age of the air hero. Charles A. Lindbergh, whose solo transatlantic flight in May 1927 sparked a revival of interest in aviation among the public, became the prototypical air hero of the 1930s. This attention was extended to the pilots who had fought in the Great War. Although a great deal of biographical literature had been written by the pilots themselves, much of it had been forgotten by time of Lindbergh's flight. Chilling accounts of the exploits of fictional pilots filled such magazines as *Aces, Flying Aces, Wings, G-8 and His Battle Aces, Sky Fighters, War Birds,* and *Sky Birds,* and eventually supplanted the recollections of the participants themselves.

Despite the popularity of the air-war pulps, Hollywood created the most lasting manifestation of the heroic pilot image in the late 1920s and 1930s. Geographer David Lowenthal asserts that "famous film representations of historic features and events are more recognizable and convincing than the authentic, original lineaments. Many viewers seem less impressed by Charles Lindbergh's original Spirit of St. Louis in the Smithsonian Institution than by the plane Jimmy Stewart flew in the movie, for 'this, after all, is the only one they *saw* crossing the ocean on film.'"[6]

If popular culture, especially film, forges popular perceptions of historical events, then the romantic vision of the air war will linger in popular memory until it is recast in the popular culture. Film, more than any other medium, is responsible for our perceptions of the World War I aviator, and it helped form persistent opinions about the chivalry and gallantry of the air war.

Wings, which appeared in 1927, began the long tradition of World War I aviation films that glorify the exploits of the combat pilot. The cinematic stereotype presented by *Wings* was so widely accepted that the *New York Times* reviewed it as docudrama in August 1927:

> This feature gives one an unforgettable idea of the existence of these daring fighters—how they were called upon at all hours of the day and night to soar into the skies and give battle to enemy planes: their lighthearted eagerness to enter the fray and also their reckless conduct once they set foot on earth for a time in the dazzling life of the French capital.[7]

To some extent, the cinematic stereotype depicted by *Wings* and its successors was true. Such aerial "aces" (pilots with considerable victories over enemy aircraft) as Britain's Albert Ball, Canada's William A. "Billy" Bishop, Germany's Manfred von Richthofen, France's Georges Guynemer, and the United States' Edward V. "Eddie" Rickenbacker accounted for an astonishing number of aerial kills and were legitimately lionized as combat heroes. In reality, a more concerted group effort soon replaced that of the highly individualistic aces. As British military historian John Terraine points out, the aces, who had "built up a mystique of aerial war which amounted almost to a religion... soon became anachronisms as air warfare left the mystical phase and entered the phase of numbers and scientific method. Formation flying was born out of the successes of the early 'aces'—mutual protection to counteract their prowess."[8]

The reckless conduct of the World War I aviator after completing a mission or patrol or while on leave is a myth. According to Denis Winter, a historian who has examined the memoirs of World War I fighter pilots, "quietness was the norm after an active patrol. Some men would go straight for a bathe in the squadron pool; others spend a quiet hour unwinding in the armoury by filling ammunition belts. Few in the mess would talk of their experiences in the face of such an urgent need for rest." Winter continues that while horseplay and "communal absorption of alcohol" were used to relieve tension in the Royal Flying Corps, these activities were to a large degree institutionalized and invariably presided over by the squadron commander.[9]

Yet the stereotypes are what persist in the popular memory. Though most of the stars and the directors of these films are long since dead, the mystique of the World War I pilot lives on, on late-night television and videotape.

The images that World War I–aviation films portray, however, are at least one step closer to reality than those of contemporary popular culture. As the actual events of the air war become more distant in memory, they become more trivialized. Thus, toys, games, cartoons, records, apparel, along with theme restaurants and speciality foods, use images of Great War aviation that are entirely detached from its actuality. It is through such media that real wartime experience, as George Mosse suggests, is "distorted and manipulated at will."[10]

Fear and Faith: The Doctrine of Strategic Bombing

In *The Rise of American Air Power*, Michael Sherry offers a plausible explanation for the perpetuation of the heroic stereotype of World War I aviation: "heroes of the air seemed lifted out of war altogether, serving as much-wanted reminders of the individual's continued significance in the machine age." At the same time,

"they appeared as throwbacks to an age of more gallant warfare, their courage magnified by the frailty of their machines and the odds against their survival." But, Sherry says, "given these images, it was easy to ignore the potential of airpower for 'scientific murder.'"[11]

Harnessing the destructive potential of air power to appropriate war goals was the theoretical basis for strategic bombing, which was developed during the interwar years and put to use in World War II. This doctrine, much of it based on the inaccurate memory (or deliberate misrepresentation) of the indecisive but psychologically effective Great War strategic bombing campaign, structured the Allied bombing campaigns of World War II.

Strategic bombing—using aircraft to attack an enemy's cities, industries, and civilian population—had been foreseen even before the advent of powered flight. By the outbreak of World War I, fear of aerial attack was widespread and occasionally hysterical, particularly in London and Paris, which were accessible and therefore vulnerable to attack by German airships. Fear of attack by airship even extended to the United States, where German zeppelins were reportedly sighted over New York on several occasions.

By 1918 practically every participant in the war had carried out some form of strategic bombing. Although the physical effects of the attacks were relatively slight, the psychological and political effects were immediate and far-reaching. For the first time in history, the threat of aerial assault, foreseen even before powered flight, had been realized: civilians had been attacked. Although moral, political, and technological factors initially limited attacks on civilian targets, desperation to end the war and desire for retaliation eventually escalated attacks against civilian populations and, by the end of the war, the line that had divided combatant from noncombatant had been irrevocably erased.

Air leaders in World War I seemed to have learned little from their wartime experiences: in reality, the airplane, despite the expectations placed on it, failed to measure up and had little effect on the war's outcome. These failures made the air prophets—Guilio Douhet in Italy, Hugh Trenchard in Great Britain, and William "Billy" Mitchell in the United States—emphasize the most effective uses for the airplane, which were incorporated into a myth about how air power, in the form of strategic bombing, could ultimately be decisive.

Unlike other modern weapons used in World War I, the airplane had a distinctly romantic aura about it (based on the false perception that it operated in an environment that was separate from what was happening on the ground) setting it apart from other military technology. For this reason, air power, it was thought, could by itself prevent another protracted ground war in which millions would be senselessly slaughtered. Moreover, faith in air power drove the air prophets in the interwar years to begin crusading for its use in future wars. These prophets were in great part responsible for convincing the public and the air planners of the interwar years that the airplane could destroy an enemy's means of production and will to fight, and force unconditional surrender.

The corrective corollary to faith in air power was fear of the destructive capacity of aerial bombardment and the attempt to prohibit its use. The armistice of November 1918 required Germany to surrender to the Allies many kinds of weapons, including the Fokker D.VII fighter and the bombers that had conducted nighttime raids on London and Paris. The Treaty of Versailles was the first of many postwar attempts to limit the use of aircraft as weapons, although its primary goal was to restrict Germany's rearmament. The Hague Conference that ran from December 1922 to February 1923 made further attempts to restrict the use of aircraft as weapons.[12]

At the Hague Conference, the Commission of Jurists, legal specialists from the United States, Great Britain, France, Italy, Japan, and the Netherlands, issued a set of precepts called "Rules of Aerial Warfare," five of which related to aerial bombardment. The code of air warfare, which came to be known as the Hague Draft Rules, attempted to prohibit aerial bombardment "for the purpose of terrorizing the civilian population, of destroying or damaging private property not of a military character, or of injuring non-combatants." It further stated that "aerial bombardment is legitimate only when directed exclusively at... military forces; military works; military establishments or depots; factories constituting important and well-known centres engaged in the manufacture of arms, ammunition, or distinctively military supplies; lines of communication or transportation used for military purposes." It outlawed the "bombardment of cities, towns, villages, dwellings, or buildings not in the immediate neighbourhood of the operations of land forces," and it forbade bombardment "in cases where the

objectives ... are so situated that they cannot be bombarded without the indiscriminate bombardment of the civilian population." These rules were, however, were never ratified and thus did not have the force of law. They were, however, voluntarily adhered to in the early months of World War II.[13]

Despite the attempts to outlaw it, there was an inevitability about aerial bombardment that cut across the faith in and fear of the bomber. Throughout the 1920s, the Royal Air Force employed what was euphemistically called "Air Control"—the bombing of hostile villages—in policing the British Empire in the Middle East. Although this tactic was not strategic bombing per se, it was an exercise in air terrorism intended to keep order and to provide a role for the Royal Air Force in peacetime. In 1931 the Japanese launched aerial attacks on Mukden and several other cities in their drive to occupy Manchuria. The following year, units of the Japanese army and navy bombed Chaipei, an eight-square-mile area in Shanghai, killing thousands of civilians.[14]

In November 1932, on the eve of the Geneva Disarmament Conference, a last-ditch attempt to prohibit aerial bombardment that ultimately collapsed, British Prime Minister Stanley Baldwin, lamenting society's vulnerability to aerial weapons and its inability to restrict them, told members of Parliament that failure to ban the bomber would mean the end of civilization in Europe. Whether or not it was true, Baldwin's famous statement, that it was "well also for the man in the street to realise that there is no power on earth that can protect him from being bombed...the bomber will always get through," legitimized the threat to civilian populations. The ethical line that distinguished civilians from combatants had been crossed in World War I and now there was no turning back.[15]

Yet the notion that air power alone could win the next war differed greatly from the actual experience of the air campaign in World War I. Edgar S. Gorrell, an officer in the U.S. Air Service during the war, collected evidence that was ignored in favor of the more seductive theory of strategic bombing. Gorrell's belief that by themselves aircraft would not be predominant in a major war was not shared by his colleagues in the Air Service (later the Army Air Corps). Advocates for air power passionately contended that an autonomous air force should be created and that the airplane would singlehandedly win the next war.

Gorrell had been directed by Chief of the

Air Service Maj. General Mason M. Patrick to compile a tactical history of American air activities during the war. His account of Air Service activities, titled *The Final Report of the Chief of Air Service AEF*, was completed early in 1919. It consisted of nineteen chapters divided into three sections dealing with combat, organizational development, logistics, training, and accomplishments.[16]

On the eve of World War II, Gorrell, now a civilian, looked back on his efforts with disappointment. He once believed that "his" history, which runs to 280 volumes, with thousands of photographs, charts, and tabulations, would be required reading for air officers and that they would profit "by the lessons learned and the mistakes made by those who had pioneered." Inaccessible and little-used, the work was relegated to "the vaults of the War Department in Washington, some of the pages torn, some yellowing, many hard to read." Sadly, valuable insights about air power in the Great War were discarded in favor of hyperbole about the efficacy of a concerted strategic bombing campaign that would bring the enemy to its knees and bring about a swift and decisive victory.[17]

Thus, the advocates of air power won out over both those who attempted to prohibit its use and those who encouraged strategists to look realistically at the lessons learned from the first major employment of the airplane in wartime. In the United States, the adherents of Billy Mitchell in the Army Air Corps, oblivious of Gorrell's findings, carried on his crusade for air power and an independent air force.

In *Arms and Men: A Study in American Military History*, Walter Millis describes the plans and goals of these men between the wars: "Independent power and authority came first; to attain the goal it was next necessary to develop a 'doctrine' which would make it militarily valid; finally, with the doctrine established, it was necessary to invent a weapon which would justify the strategy." The new doctrine was called precision bombing and it was based on the concepts established by Mitchell, Trenchard, Douhet, and their devotees.[18]

The doctrine of precision bombing did not advocate indiscriminate attacks but those targeted at a few key components, especially the enemy's economic institutions, whose destruction would disrupt the functioning of the entire state and cause the enemy's will to fight to collapse.[19]

In turn, the doctrine of precision bombing was translated into a weapon—the Boeing B-17 bomber with the Norden bombsight, which would facilitate the execution of the doctrine by enabling bombing crews to drop their bombs with pinpoint precision and exactness. Yet, in truth, both these developments were cloaked in subterfuge. The B-17 was promoted by the Air Corps as a defensive weapon designed specifically for "coastal defense" and the Norden bombsight was oversold before its true accuracy could be determined. (It may be no accident that the bombsight's top security designation prohibited a true analysis of its ability to perform its task.)[20]

The Combined Bomber Offensive, prescribed by the Casablanca Conference of January 1943, in which bombers of the U.S. Army Air Forces and the Royal Air Force would attack targets in Germany both by day and night, was the first real opportunity for the United States to test the theory of precision bombing. The American raids were to take place in daylight hours and were directed toward specific industrial targets such as aircraft factories, the ball-bearing industry, and oil-production installations. The British night attacks were directed primarily at German cities, with little regard to the damage inflicted on civilians.[21]

By the middle of 1944, however, precision bombing had been abandoned, the result of disastrous American losses: in July 1943 at Ploesti, Romania, more than one-third of the B-24 Liberators dispatched from North Africa failed to return; in August 1943, at Schweinfurt and Regensburg, Germany, sixty of the 376 B-17s attacking the targets were lost; and again at Schweinfurt in October 1943, sixty of the 291 attacking B-17s were shot down. The American losses were the result of sharpened German air defenses and an aggressive Luftwaffe. With the demonstrated inaccuracy of "precison bombardment," which failed to produce the desired results, the United States changed its bombing strategy to direct attacks that would affect German morale and bring a quick end to the war.[22]

In Japan, the situation was similar. Early precision raids carried out by Boeing B-29 Superfortresses were directed toward the Japanese aircraft-engine industry, particularly the Musashi engine plant in Tokyo. But bad weather reduced the effectiveness of these raids and others on strategic targets. According to historian Lee Kennett, in three months of bombing high-priority targets, "not a single one had been destroyed. No more than 10 percent of the bombs dropped seemed to be landing near the objective."[23]

As in Europe, precision bombing was abandoned in favor of incendiary attacks on Japanese cities. One particular raid, the attack on Tokyo on March 9-10, 1945, was particularly devastating. Kennett calculates that 83,793 persons were killed, although the figure may be closer to 100,000. "The vast fires," Kennett writes, "burned out some sixteen square miles of the immense city and destroyed a quarter of a million structures. ... Worst of all, that night the *Akakaze*, or 'Red Wind,' was blowing across Tokyo, and it took the flames with it. ... A tidal wave of fire moved across the city, the flames preceded by superheated vapors that felled anyone that breathed them."[24]

The atomic bomb attacks on Hiroshima and Nagasaki in August 1945 were the culmination of the strategic bombing offensive in Japan. In Hiroshima, the atom bomb vaporized four square miles of the city. Some 48,000 buildings were completely demolished, and 70,000 more were damaged or destroyed. Although the total number of deaths is still unknown, it is estimated that out of a total population of 320,000 civilians and military, 80,000 died as a result of the initial blast; many others were later killed by injury or radiation. Japanese estimates place the number of deaths by December 1945 at 140,000, plus or minus 10,000.[25]

Although the atomic bomb attacks helped bring about the unconditional surrender of the Japanese, the price paid in human life, the ethical considerations, and the implications for the future wholesale destruction of the world made it very costly. In Europe, the results of strategic bombing were less than conclusive. Although they estimated the British strategic air campaign to be a qualified success, Charles K. Webster and Noble Frankland wrote in their official postwar assessment of it that the huge area bombing offensive (March 1943 to March 1944) neither broke nor "significantly impaired" the "will of the German people" and that "the effect on war production was remarkably small." In the United States, opinions varied widely on the effectiveness of strategic bombing in Europe: its advocates claimed considerable accomplishment in bringing Germany to its knees; its detractors claimed that it failed to bring about a prompt German surrender and cost too much in terms of lost air crews and aircraft.[26]

The Long Shadow of Strategic Bombing

Today, three generations later, we still live with the consequences of World War I in the air. The bombing of civilian targets with the intention of destroying the enemy's morale and will to resist, carried out for the first time in that war, laid the groundwork for what was to come. Since the end of World War II, civilians have had to live with the fear of aerial attack and, far worse, of nuclear destruction from the air. Since the advent of the missile age, the human race has had the potential to destroy the entire planet many times over with nuclear weapons.

In July 1990, *Time* magazine reported that only one of the nearly two hundred nuclear warheads on board the U.S. missile submarine *Tennessee* "would be enough to flatten the Kremlin and every building within half a mile if detonated 6,000 ft. over Moscow. Up to two miles from ground zero, all but the toughest structures would be destroyed, and even as far as four miles away, wood and brick buildings would collapse and burst into flames." Additionally, *Time* noted that "if no more than a third of the current U.S. arsenal of 12,000 warheads made it through the Soviet defenses, the nuclear punch would pulverize every Soviet city with a population of more than 25,000." Yet, instead of disarmament, military planners advocate existing or increased levels of response.[27]

In 1991 the dismantling of the Soviet empire made it apparent that the Cold War had ended. Yet, the U.S. Air Force still argues vociferously for development of the B-2 bomber, even though the cost of development and production has skyrocketed to billions of dollars.

If we have not yet come to accept the inevitability of nuclear destruction, we have indeed seen death come from the sky. A U.S. Census Bureau analyst estimated that 70,000 civilians were killed as an aftermath of the bombing campaign in the recent Gulf War. (The Pentagon remains silent on this issue.) The debate over the effectiveness of strategic bombing continues unabated, with the Air Force contending that its laser-guided bombs were more accurate, deadly, and humane, since they were directed toward strategic targets, and its critics asserting that while that may be the case, conventional bombs dropped on Iraq fell miles from their targets. Wherever the truth lies, the fact remains that innocent civilians died as a result of the bombing and that governments on all sides, in their eagerness to demonstrate the latest developments in military technology, are unrepentant.[28]

Yet, the fanciful conception of air combat, first promulgated in the skies over the Western Front, distorted beyond recognition of its true value, made meaningless by being trivialized in toys, games, and the kitsch of everyday life, and disconnected from its origins, is the preferred memory of the air war. The true and more deadly consequences of aerial warfare remain hidden behind clouds of official obfuscation, while ordinary citizens go about their business. As T.S. Eliot pointed out in his poem "Burnt Norton," "human kind/Cannot bear very much reality."[29]

1. A German general writing to his wife, quoted in Keith Robbins, *The First World War* (Oxford: Oxford University Press, 1985), 88.

2. George L. Mosse, *Fallen Soldiers: Reshaping the Memory of the World Wars* (New York: Oxford University Press, 1990), 7.

3. Edward M. Coffman, *The War to End All Wars: The American Military Experience in World War I* (Madison: University of Wisconsin Press, 1986), 187.

4. David Thelen, ed., *Memory and American History* (Bloomington: Indiana University Press, 1990), vii.

5. Adapted from Patricke Johns-Heinke and Hans H. Gerth, "Values in Mass Periodical Fiction, 1921-1940," *The Public Opinion Quarterly*, Spring 1949, 105. Johns-Heinke and Gerth argue that periodical fiction shapes values; subsequent writers have examined the effects of other mass media like popular films, books, television programs, advertising, etc., on public values.

6. David Lowenthal, "The Timeless Past: Some Anglo-American Historical Preconceptions," in *Memory and American History*, 138.

7. "The Flying Fighters," [anon. review of *Wings*] reprinted in *The New York Times Directory of the Film* (New York: Arno Press, 1971), 26.

8. John Terraine, *White Heat: The New Warfare, 1914-1918* (London: Sidgwick & Jackson, 1982), 198.

9. Denis Winter, *The First of the Few: Fighter Pilots of the First World War* (Athens: University of Georgia Press, 1983), 109, 185-89.

10. Mosse, 7.

11. Michael S. Sherry, *The Rise of American Air Power: The Creation of Armageddon* (New Haven: Yale University Press, 1987), 39.

12. Lee Kennett, *A History of Strategic Bombing* (New York: Charles Scribner's Sons, 1982), 61.

13. Kennett, 63-67.

14. Robert Goralski, *World War II Almanac, 1931-1945: A Political and Military Record* (New York: Bonanza Books, 1984), 2, 10.

15. Kennett, 68-69; Baldwin quoted in N. H. Gibbs, *History of the Second World War*: Grand Strategy, vol. 1, Rearmament Policy (London: Her Majesty's Stationery Office, 1976, 553-54.

16. Maurer, Maurer, ed., *The U.S. Air Service in World War I*, vol. 1, The Final Report and A Tactical History (Washington, D.C.: The Office of Air Force History,

1978), 4, 8. According to Maurer (vol. 1, 10, 9, vii), the tactical history, officially titled *A Tactical History of the Air Service, AEF*, was partially published in an Air Service Information Circular in 1920. *The Final Report of the Chief of the Air Service, AEF* was first published on February 15, 1921, in volume 2, no. 180, of the Air Service Information Circular (Aviation), and by the U.S. Army's Historical Division in 1948, in a compilation of documents titled *United States Army in the World War, 1917-1919*. Both the *Tactical History* and the *Final Report* appeared together for the first time in 1978 in the first volume of *The U.S. Air Service in World War I*.

17. Edgar S. Gorrell, "The Measure of America's World War Aeronautical Effort," Norwich University, Publication No. 6, November 26, 1940, v-vi; Maurer, 10. Gorrell's history is now in the collection of the National Archives and is available on 58 reels of microfilm.

18. Walter Millis, *Arms and Men: A Study in American Military History* (New York: Putnam, 1956), 231, quoted in Sherry, 50.

19. Sherry, 51.

20. Kennett, 88.

21. Kennett, 145.

22. Kennett, 153, 160-61.

23. Kennett, 168-69.

24. Kennett, 171.

25. William A. Manchester, *The Glory and the Dream: A Narrative History of America, 1932-1972* (New York: Bantam Books, 1980), 382; Richard Rhodes, *The Making of the Atomic Bomb* (New York: Simon and Schuster, 1988), 728; Gordon Thomas and Max Morgan Witts, *Ruin from the Air: The Atomic Mission to Hiroshima* (London: Hamish Hamilton, 1977), 323; John Newhouse, *War and Peace in the Nuclear Age* (New York: Vintage Books, 1990), 50; *A Brief Summary of the Atomic Bombing and its Effects* (Hiroshima: Hiroshima Peace Memorial Museum, 1989), 24.

26. Charles Webster and Noble Frankland, *The Strategic Air Offensive Against Germany*, Vol. 3: Victory, Part 5 (London: Her Majesty's Stationery Office, 1961), 288.

27. Bruce van Voorst, "America's Doomsday Machine," *Time*, July 16, 1990, 19.

28. "70,000 Iraqis Said to Have Died Post-War," *The Washington Post*, January 9, 1992.

29. T.S. Eliot, *Collected Poems, 1909-1962* (New York: Harcourt Brace Jovanovich, 1963, 176.

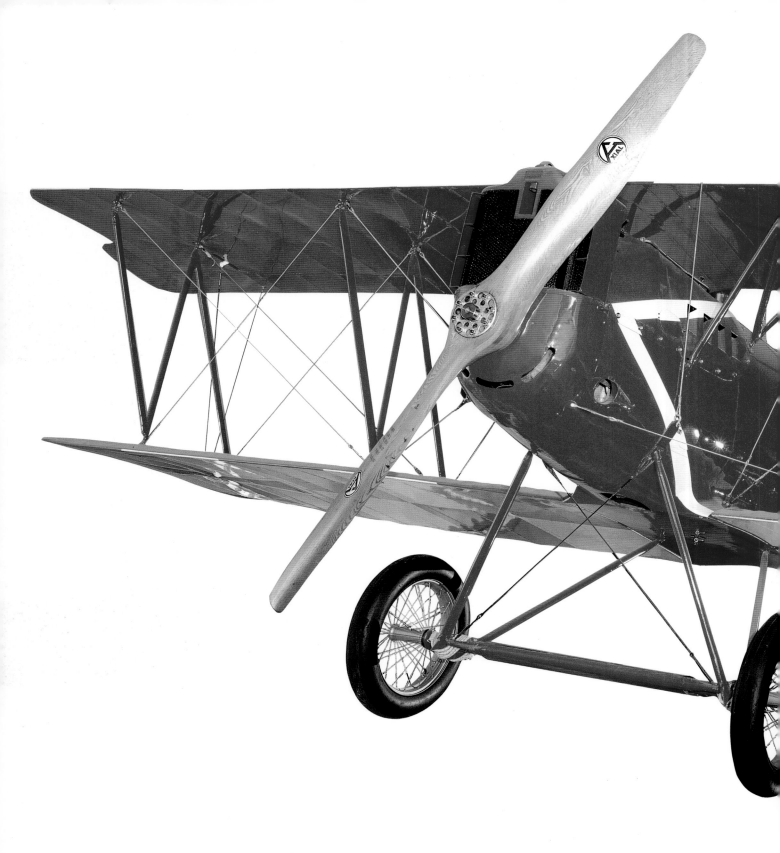

I Remembering the Great War in the Air

MORE THAN SEVENTY YEARS AFTER the fighting ceased, images drawn from World War I are still prevalent in American culture. In toy stores around the country, stuffed teddy bears are clothed to appear like World War I pilots; games give players the opportunity to pit themselves against the aces of 1914–1918 in mock dogfights in which victory is determined by spinning a dial, rolling a marble, or moving quickly around the spaces of a playing board. In the pages of comics and on television specials, Snoopy continues to battle his greatest foe, the Red Baron.

PFALZ D-XII

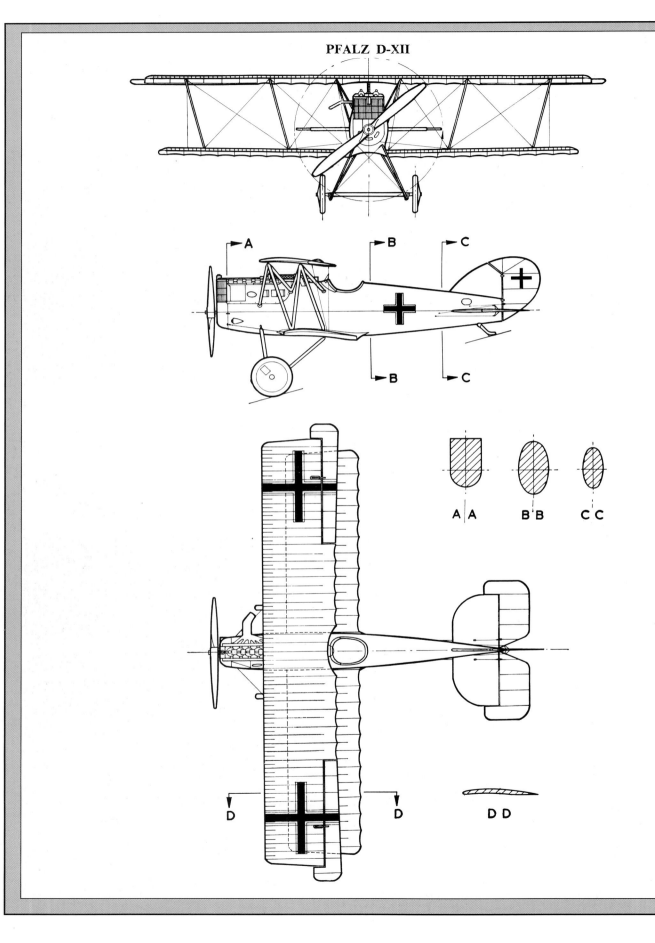

Pfalz D.XII:
Battlefront Success and Hollywood Star

The National Air and Space Museum's German Pfalz D.XII fighter logged more hours flying in Hollywood aviation films than it did during the war. During the 1930s these films helped shape perceptions of the air war and perpetuate the image of the World War I pilot as a chivalrous "knight of the air." For its role in the 1930 film *The Dawn Patrol*, the Pfalz D.XII was repainted an historically inaccurate red color, and a distinctive skull-and-crossbones motif was applied on its fuselage. In the film, it was flown by the fictitious ace von Richter, a stereotypically fearsome German fighter pilot.

The Pfalz D.XII first appeared on the Western Front in mid-August 1918. It was built as a replacement for the outdated Albatros D.Va, the Fokker Dr.I triplane, and earlier Pfalz designs. The wartime history of this particular aircraft is obscure. After the war it was one of two Pfalz D.XII's brought to this country as part of Allied war reparations.

In 1928 it was purchased as war surplus and brought to Hollywood for use in the 1930 version of *The Dawn Patrol*. Howard Hughes later purchased it for his 1930 film *Hell's Angels*. The aircraft was stored on a back lot, then acquired by Louis C. Kennell, property manager for Paramount Pictures, and prepared for use in the 1938 version of *The Dawn Patrol* but never flown. The Smithsonian Institution later acquired the aircraft and refurbished it for use in *Legend, Memory and the Great War in the Air*.

A captured Pfalz D.XII photographed on an Allied airfield shortly after the end of hostilities. This aircraft may be the Pfalz D.XII now in the National Air and Space Museum's collection.

CURSE YOU, RED BARON!

© 1965 United Feature Syndicate, Inc.   SCHULZ

Snoopy's continuing battle with the cursed "Red Baron" is indicative of how deeply that myth is ingrained in American culture.

Fanciful and completely disconnected from the grim reality of life and death in the air, this imagery gives a simplified and biased view of a complex historical event. For example, the fighter aces remain the war's most celebrated heroes, even though most World War I fliers were neither fighter pilots nor aces and aerial combat had little effect on the outcome of the war. The representations of World War I aviation seen in the graphics of the board games and comic strips lack historical accuracy; instead, they embody a romantic and ultimately appealing version of the war. The popularity of this glamorized and sanitized portrayal of air war provides insight into how historical events are remembered.

The Red Baron: 1918 to the Present

Propaganda, popular literature, Hollywood films, and the passage of time have all helped shape our perception of aviation's role during World War I. Today, German ace Manfred von Richthofen's name and image are commonly associated with heroism and chivalry. The legend

Perhaps the most bizarre example of the perpetuation of the "knights of the air" mythos was the Cockburn-Lange photographic hoax, concocted by Wesley Archer, who was a Royal Flying Corps pilot. The action-packed Cockburn-Lange photographs, which appeared in 1932, purported to show aerial combat in World War I as it really was. Although they have long been discredited by historians and photographic experts, these photographs are still being used to illustrate historical textbooks. Using models of wartime aircraft, Wesley Archer created dogfight tableaux and photographed each scene. He then superimposed the images of the models on a composite background and photographed the collage. The resultant photographs were impressive but bogus.

Pizza companies, rock-music groups, and import companies have all employed the Red Baron to sell their products.

In 1969 the rock group Led Zeppelin adapted this photograph of Manfred von Richthofen's squadron for the cover artwork of its second album.

Popular culture rarely concentrates on von Richthofen's life outside of World War I. Born to a landed family, he served with an elite German cavalry unit before he became a pilot.

Since the publication of Floyd Gibbons's *The Red Knight of Germany* in 1927, new titles have continually added to the mass of popular literature about von Richthofen, shaping the legend of the Red Baron to this day.

Printed on the cheapest paper available, the pulp magazines of the late 1920s and 1930s helped shape a generation's perceptions about World War I flying.

of the man whom the British named the "Red Baron" is one of the most durable and influential memories of World War I. Long before the war ended, however, wartime propaganda campaigns had already begun the metamorphosis of the man into a living legend.

Although von Richthofen did not survive to the conclusion of the Great War, German newspapers and propaganda office had already publicized the ace's exploits. Many knew that he had scored eighty victories and imagined that he had shot down his victims in the midst of dramatic dogfights. In fact, he often used stealth and surprise to make quick kills. Because he died on April 21, 1918, in the cockpit of a red Fokker Dr.I triplane, it was often assumed that he had won most of his victories in this aircraft. He actually scored only nineteen of his eighty victories in the Dr.I.

During the war, the German government's recognition of von Richthofen's exploits established him as a national hero. His death in combat endowed him with mythic stature in the minds of his countrymen and enemies alike. Even in the United States, young boys, including Charles A. Lindbergh, were taken with the German war hero. The transatlantic pilot's account of his childhood fascination with the flying aces of World War I reveals that this interest was stoked by numerous newspaper reports on the topic. In his book, *Autobiography of Values,* Lindbergh wrote, "After the war started, I searched newspapers for reports of aerial combats—articles about Fonck, Mannock, Bishop, Richthofen, and Rickenbacker.... Attacking enemy fighters, bombers, and balloons in mortal combat, [they] represented chivalry and daring in my own day as did King Arthur's knights in childhood stories."

The legend of the Red Baron, however, was not just a wartime phenomenon. During the interwar years, popular authors perpetuated the myth. In his best-selling book, *The Red Knight of Germany*, Floyd Gibbons portrayed von Richthofen's life as the romantic saga of a modern-day hero. Although he based the book on official sources, Gibbons interpreted the facts in a highly fictionalized manner. Gibbons's depiction of von Richthofen's attitude toward combat flying is representative of the author's intuitive style: "He fought fair, hard, and to kill, and the better his foeman fought to kill him, the better he liked him for it." Many youths of the 1920s and 1930s learned about the Red Baron and the war in the air from these exaggerated accounts.

The Interwar Years: Pulps, Comic Books, and Hollywood Films

The events of the interwar years had a great influence on our memory of World War I. Charles Lindbergh's 1927 transatlantic flight helped to fuel a resurgent interest in all aviators including the World War I aces. In addition to such novels as Gibbons's *The Red Knight of Germany*, pulp magazines, comic books, and Hollywood films all glorified aerial combat. Aviation enthusiasts built models of fighter aircraft and reenacted the dogfights of the war with miniature reproductions. They learned about the air war from reading pulp novels and pilot memoirs, listening to radio dramas, and watching movies.

The romantic, chivalric view of the air war was often presented to the public in the form of pilot memoirs, many of which were published between 1914 and 1918. Some were touching and sensitive descriptions of what it was like to fight in the air or what the psychological effects of air combat were. Most, however, were filled with highly charged accounts of the adventure and excitement of air combat. One of the highest-scoring Allied aces, William A. "Billy" Bishop, for example, wrote in his memoir: "CHIVALRY! Of course it existed! The bitterness and hatred between the armies and navies engaged in the War, as well as the intense feeling of the civilians, was not present in the Air Forces of the countries involved. In its place was a healthy respect for and interest in the opposing flying men."

Some writers, like Elliott White Springs, also an ace, took a different approach, not as sentimental but no less romantic. In his novel, *War Birds: Diary of an Unknown Aviator*, Springs deals with the darker aspects of combat flying and the physical and emotional toll it takes on the pilot. He informed his reader that "the average life at the front was forty-eight hours in the air," a grim projection. However, this knowledge did nothing but whet the appetite of the aspiring ace. "No man who has ever pressed triggers above the bright blue sky will ever be happy keeping books," Springs confided.

Various histories and memoirs were published about the legendary World War I French fighter squadron N.124, the Lafayette Escadrille, which was composed of U.S. volunteers in the service of the French. Some say the Escadrille primarily attracted patriotic young men from prominent families, who felt strongly that the United States should abandon its neutral position and join the Allied cause. Others contend it was made up of freewheeling, wealthy young adventurers eager for the thrill of combat. The Lafayette Escadrille, despite its disputed origins, undoubtedly molded public perceptions about the gallantry and daring of the men who fought the air war in France. One measure of the prestige that members of the Lafayette Escadrille enjoyed was that by 1930 more than 4,000 men had falsely claimed to have been one of its members!

The so-called pulps, magazines printed on paper made from cheap wood pulp, which appeared in the late 1920s and prospered well into the 1930s, presented another side of the World War I aviator. In the popular press, military pilots were portrayed as rough-and-ready adventurers with a bent toward brutality. The overly dramatic and highly suspect descriptions of aerial combat were written with sales, not accuracy, in mind.

Hollywood Knights

Hollywood films produced during the years between World Wars I and II played a greater role in establishing the legend of the "knights of the air" than any other medium. The romantic image of the aviator portrayed in these films is remarkably persistent and has shaped our perception of the war in the air to the present day.

The World War I aviation craze in Hollywood was part of a larger cultural fascination with flying that began with Charles Lindbergh's transatlantic flight. *Wings*, the 1927 film, was the first air epic and the first film to win an Academy Award for best motion picture. Films were a natural canvas for simulating the air war; they could liberate words from the pages of a book and visually recreate the aerial battles of World War I with real airplanes. The public responded favorably, and a film genre was born.

After *Wings* came *Lilac Time* (1928), *Hell's Angels* (1930), and two versions of *The Dawn Patrol* (1930 and 1938), to name a few. In each of these films, Hollywood's depiction of the air war focused largely on adventure and aerial

Wings (1927) inaugurated a series of nearly two dozen films on the theme of World War I aviation produced in Hollywood during an eleven-year period that ended with the onset of World War II. *The Dawn Patrol*, first released in 1930 and remade with a new cast in 1938, proved one of the most popular.

action and often idealized the darker side of aerial combat—fatigue, mental stress, killing, and dying. The plots of most World War I aviation films made during the 1930s are remarkably similar, with stock characters, contrived plots, love triangles, spies, and other improbable situations. Yet moviegoers would sit through any of these hackneyed scenes if the aerial sequences were spectacular enough.

World War II brought to an end Hollywood's chronicle of the Great War in the air and generated a new style of aerial war film that was quite different from what had gone before. But the World War I aviation film did not die out entirely. In 1956 the director of *Wings*, William Wellman, attempted to revive the World War I air war film in *The Lafayette Escadrille*. In the 1960s and 1970s other World War I flying movies, including *The Blue Max*, *von Richthofen and Brown*, and *Darling Lili*, were brought to the silver screen, but the genre had long since lost its popular appeal.

The heroic image of the fighter pilot—as depicted by such movies as *Top Gun*—remains in vogue today. Jet fighter pilots now fly at more than twice the speed of sound and can shoot down enemy aircraft beyond visual range. But the romanticized human role depicted in films is remarkably similar to the image of fighter pilots that originated during World War I.

The Legacy

The aviator emerged from World War I as a genuine hero—the embodiment of traditional values, beliefs, and ideals. The nineteenth-century notion of honor and chivalry in battle had been mortally wounded in the trenches along with the millions of men killed in the slaughter, but the aviator, who fought his battles hand-to-hand high above the mass killing on the ground, was seen as a breed apart. In a war where there were no traditional soldier heroes, the aviator was revered for his daring exploits and celebrated by emperors, politicians, and the public.

David Lloyd George, the Prime Minister of Great Britain during World War I, for example, extolled the chivalric virtues of pilots in a wartime speech, and thus helped to bring about their glorification:

> The heavens are their battlefield; they are the Cavalry of the clouds. High above the squalor and the mud, so high in the firmament that they are not visible from the earth, they fight out the eternal issues of right and wrong....Every flight is a romance; every report is an epic. They are the knighthood of the war, without fear and without reproach. They recall the old legends of chivalry, not merely the daring of their exploits, but by the nobility of their spirit, and amongst the multitudes of heroes, let us think of the chivalry of the air.

Popular culture of the 1920s and 1930s perpetuated and elaborated on the myth of the ace and his role in combat. During the past decades the popular perception of World War I has strayed even further from the reality of the war. In the 1990s heroic images of biplanes and fighter pilots that originated more than seventy years ago are still used to sell products such as neckties and pizza to consumers who barely realize their connection with the war.

The evolution of the popular perception of aviation's role in World War I reveals how legend colors the memory of an event. The myths of the "knights of the air," born during World War I, have formed the basis for commonly held attitudes about the first major war in the air. In fact, these myths have influenced the planning and use of air power during the World War II and are still with us today.

II An Illusion of Glory: The Origins of the Fighter Ace Legend

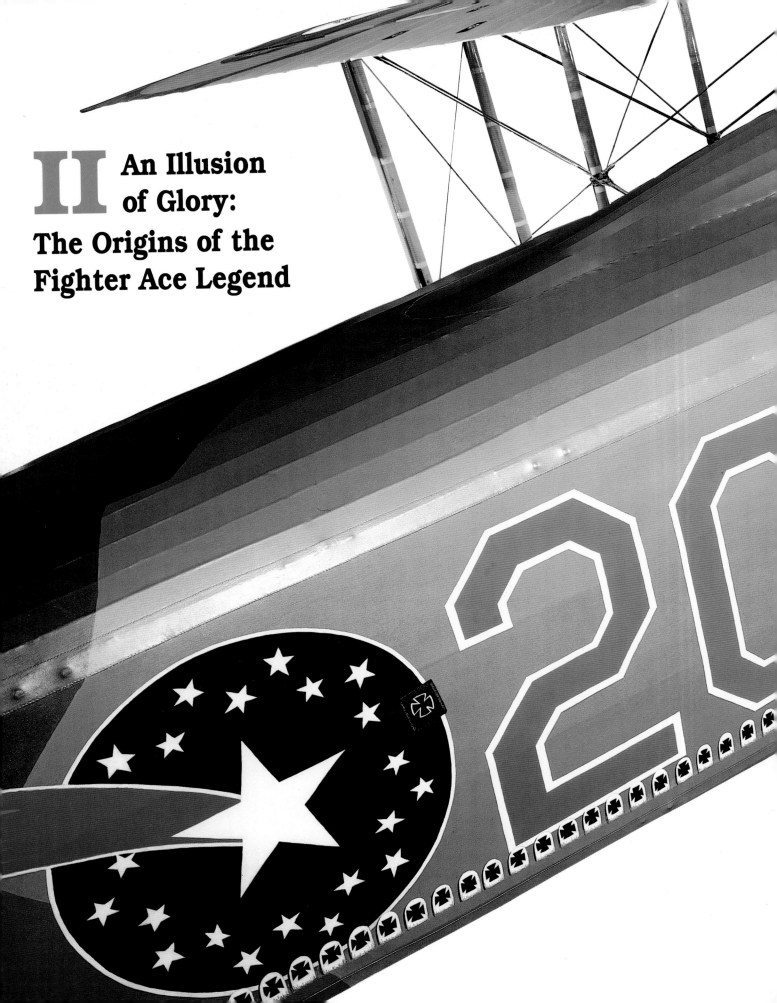

"This man...carried alone a responsibility as great as that of the mighty Generals behind the lines."

LIEUTENANT SCOTT MORGAN, *THE LONE EAGLE FIGHTING ACE,* 1938 NOVEL.

The Ace Is Born

THE MOST ENDURING STEREOTYPE of aerial combat created in World War I was that of the "ace," a fighter pilot who gained his reputation by shooting down enemy aircraft. Contrary to the image created by such novelists as Scott Morgan, however, the ace's combat role was not as vital as that of the "mighty Generals behind the lines."

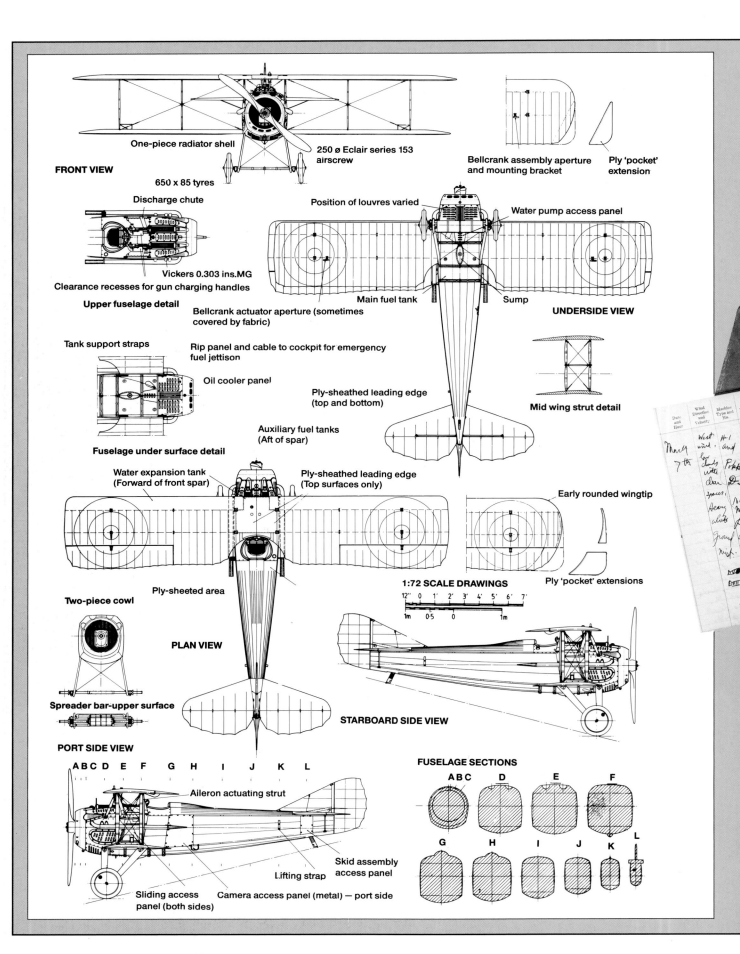

FRONT VIEW

One-piece radiator shell

250 ø Eclair series 153 airscrew

650 x 85 tyres

Discharge chute

Vickers 0.303 ins.MG

Clearance recesses for gun charging handles

Upper fuselage detail

Bellcrank actuator aperture (sometimes covered by fabric)

Tank support straps

Rip panel and cable to cockpit for emergency fuel jettison

Oil cooler panel

Fuselage under surface detail

Bellcrank assembly aperture and mounting bracket

Ply 'pocket' extension

Position of louvres varied

Water pump access panel

Main fuel tank

Sump

UNDERSIDE VIEW

Ply-sheathed leading edge (top and bottom)

Auxiliary fuel tanks (Aft of spar)

Mid wing strut detail

Water expansion tank (Forward of front spar)

Ply-sheathed leading edge (Top surfaces only)

Early rounded wingtip

Two-piece cowl

Ply-sheeted area

PLAN VIEW

1:72 SCALE DRAWINGS

12" 0 1' 2' 3' 4' 5' 6' 7'

1m 0.5 0 1m

Ply 'pocket' extensions

Spreader bar-upper surface

STARBOARD SIDE VIEW

PORT SIDE VIEW

A B C D E F G H I J K L

Aileron actuating strut

Skid assembly access panel

Lifting strap

Sliding access panel (both sides)

Camera access panel (metal) — port side

FUSELAGE SECTIONS

A B C   D   E   F

G   H   I   J   K   L

SPAD XIII:
"Smith IV"

Strong, sturdy, powerful, well-armed, and easy to fly, the SPAD (an acronym for it manufacturer, Société Pour l'Aviation et ses Dérivés) XIII was the dominant fighter flown by French, American, and Italian pilots during the last year of World War I. An improved version of the successful SPAD VII, the SPAD XIII had a more powerful engine, better armament, and aerodynamic changes that refined its control and maneuverability. About 900 of the 8,500 SPAD XIIIs built were used by the American Expeditionary Force.

American ace Arthur Raymond "Ray" Brooks of the 22nd Aero Pursuit Squadron, who flew the National Air and Space Museum's SPAD in combat, named it *Smith IV*.

The name referred to the college his fiancée attended and the fact that it was the fourth SPAD he had flown. Brooks also designed the distinctive insignia, employed to enable pilots to identify members of their squadrons, on the side of *Smith IV*'s fuselage.

The National Air and Space Museum's SPAD XIII was built by Kellner and Sons Piano Works and constructed from salvaged aircraft. On September 15, 1918, it was assigned to the 22nd Aero Pursuit Squadron of the U.S. Army Air Service, which was taking part in the Saint-Mihiel offensive. The aircraft entered combat during this campaign, and by the end of the war six victories had been scored in it by various pilots.

1. Ray Brooks, an American pilot who flew the National Air and Space Museum's SPAD XIII, commented in the pages of his logbook on his aircraft's performance.

2. The Hispano-Suiza engine that powered the French SPAD XIII was superior to the Mercedes D.IIIa used on manycontempor-ary German fighters. Because its cylinders were arranged in a V shape along the crankshaft, the "Hisso" was more compact and vibrated less than its German counterpart. Made largely of aluminum instead of steel, the Hisso was also lighter. These features and an internal carburetor heater combined to produce more horsepower. These differences helped make the SPAD XIII faster and more nimble than the Mercedes-powered German Albatros D.Va. The Hisso engine was manufactured in France by Société d'Exploitation des Materials Hispano-Suiza and other factories and produced under license in Britain, Italy, and the United States, and other companies in France.

3. To personalize their aircraft, pilots often gave them names or chose insignias that had significance to their lives outside of the war. Ray Brooks, whose fighter squadron carried this colorful emblem, claimed that on the night that the United States declared war, he had seen a shooting star.

4. The names of aces were invoked to sell the Hispano-Suiza engine. The Wright-Martin Aircraft Corporation was the only U.S. company licensed to build this engine. Because the U.S. aviation industry was not able to retool and convert from metric and British Standard to American specifications, the Wright-Martin Corporation did not produce enough engines to be sent to France before the war ended.

1

3

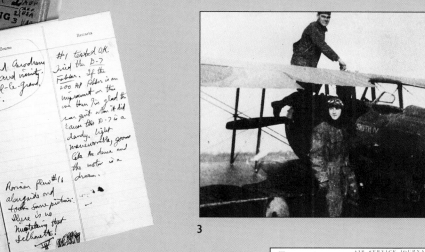

2

4

Melodramatic prints, such as "The Brilliant Prowess of Gilbert the Aviator," relied more on colorful imagery than on words to convey their moral, religious, humorous, or political message. Because they were accessible to both illiterate and literate people, they informed a broader audience than newspapers. These inexpensive and widely available images had a long history of influencing public opinion.

"And You? Subscribe to the War Loan." The governments of the combatant nations quickly recognized the advertising value of the ace image. It was used to encourage recruiting and, in this German poster of 1917, to convince the public to buy bonds to support the war effort.

This British poster from 1915 used the image of Sublieutenant R.A.J. Warneford, a Royal Naval Air Service pilot who had destroyed the German Zeppelin LZ 37, to recruit men for the infantry.

LA GUERRE 1914-1915
EN IMAGES
Faits, Combats, Episodes, Récits

– LA GUERRE DANS LES AIRS –
Brillante Prouesse de l'Aviateur GILBERT

Illustrations de G. B.
PELLERIN & Cie, imp. édit
IMAGERIE D'ÉPINAL, N°

Ce très brillant exploit fut accompli le 10 janvier 1915 près de Chaulnes alors que le pilote Gilbert et le lieutenant observateur de Puechedron venaient d'ape[r] un "Aviatik" allemand se dirigeant sur Amiens : ils lui donnèrent aussitôt la chasse et le rattrapèrent non loin de cette ville. L'observateur tira quatre bulle[s] carabine, atteignant deux fois le lieutenant von Falkenstein et blessant au cou le pilote Keller qui atterrit aussitôt. L'appareil vint choir en bon état sur le sol [...]

Und Ihr?

Zeichnet Kriegsanleihe

THE
SPORTSMAN BATTALION'S
RECRUIT
WHO WRECKED THE ZEPPELIN
and won the V.C.

By permission of F. M. Birkett and The "Daily Sketch."

FOLLOW HIS LEAD
AND JOIN THE
SPORTSMAN'S BATTALION
Apply E. CUNLIFFE-OWEN, Hotel Cecil, Strand, London,

W. STRAKER, Ltd., Printers, 13, Coventry Street, Piccadilly, W.

By war's end, the ace, in his role as a symbolic hero, had instead a direct and important impact on the morale of the men in the trenches and of the civilians on the home front. At the outbreak of the war, officials had not yet recognized the ace's intrinsic propaganda value, and pilots received little or no recognition for their efforts. Journalists, who were early advocates of the role of aviation, complained about the lack of information on the war in the air. The French press played a particularly important role in creating the heroic image of the ace. The designation "ace" supposedly originated in 1915, when a Paris newspaper eulogized Adolphe Pégoud as *"l'as de notre aviation"* (the ace of our aviation), after he had achieved his fourth victory.

Journalistic pressure was only one factor that prompted officials to identify and recognize pilots. Prominent business figures also called for special awards and distinctions. André Michelin, the French tire magnate, for example, established a million-franc fund for aviators who distinguished themselves in battle.

More important to the history of the ace was the course of the war itself. As the cost of the war of attrition increased, the opposing governments expanded their morale-raising programs to encourage public support. Few heroes, however, emerged out of the mass, anonymous slaughter in the trenches. As early as 1915, government ministries had turned to the pilot to try to boost public morale. This self-serving appropriation of the airman was the final step in transforming the prewar image of the pilot as a dashing adventurer into a romantic military hero.

Who Was the Ace?

The criteria for becoming an ace varied from country to country, but generally a minimum of five victories were enough to qualify. Early in the war, a pilot needed fewer victories to become an ace. Lt. Max Immelmann shot down only four planes but became the first German pilot to be designated with this honor. Later, when aerial combat had become commonplace, pilots had to score more victories to qualify. As a result, some began to make fraudulent claims to

Oberleutnant Immelmann

362
Postkartenvertrieb W. Sanke
BERLIN N. 32.
Nachdruck wird gerichtlich verfolgt.

By 1916 Max Immelmann, Germany's first aerial ace, had five victories to his name. To honor his latest accomplishment, German military leaders decided to award him the Pour le Mérite, Germany's most prestigious medal for officers. Immelmann's record set the standard for measuring aerial heroism during the early years of the war. By 1918 thirty victories were necessary to gain the same honor.

Silver goblets (like the one pictured at right) were presented to German aviators who distinguished themselves in combat, and in 1916 Manfred von Richthofen earned one for his first victory. For every enemy airplane he shot down, this German pilot, perhaps the war's most well-known ace, awarded himself with trophies. He collected a piece of the wreckage of the downed enemy aircraft and sent it home to his mother who would display it in his bedroom according to his instructions. Richthofen also commissioned a jeweler to make a minature silver goblet every time he scored a victory.

meet the quota. Governments imposed systems for verifying victories to ensure that all aces had earned the right to be regarded as national heroes.

Once a novice German fighter pilot had completed his flight training and earned his pilot's badge, he set his sights on the Iron Cross First Class. This decoration was awarded to pilots who were skillful (and lucky) enough to survive a certain number of missions or for acts of heroism. To claim the coveted honor Pour le Mérite, he had to shoot down a set number of enemy aircraft, a requirement that rose to thirty by 1918.

The Pour le Mérite, the most prestigious German military decoration awarded to officers, had traditionally been associated with the cavalry, infantry, and navy. Created in 1740 by Prussian King Frederick the Great, the Pour le Mérite (literally, "for merit"; so named because French was the language of the Prussian court) identified heroes in Germany's armed forces. During World War I this award, however, became associated with fighter aces. The British gave the medal the popular name "Blue Max," which referred to the award's blue-and-gold color and to Max Immelmann, the first German ace to receive it.

The Pour le Mérite had a long history, but new awards were also created to honor the ace's contributions. Silver goblets were presented to German aviators who distinguished themselves in combat. The origins of the award, however, are obscure. One story claims that the Prussian crown prince had his wedding silver melted down to provide victory goblets for national air heroes. Another claims that industrialists presented the award to each German aviator who downed an enemy aircraft. By the end of the war, the goblets were given not for one aerial victory, but for eight or nine, and were made of iron instead of silver, which had by then become scarce.

Gallant Knight and Hunter

In the eyes of civilians, infantrymen, and even the members of the flying corps, aviators fought their battles following a code of honor characterized by medieval notions of valor. This image, reminiscent of the heroics of Arthurian knights, was most frequently seen in the propaganda posters, postcards, medallions, and similar paraphernalia created for public consumption.

The popular presentation of the aerial war

Oswald Boelcke was among the first German aces to appear on the postcards produced by the Sanke company and distributed throughout Germany.

Unser Helden-Fl...
Leutnant Parsc...

Vizefeldwebel u. ...
einer unser erfolgreichsten Balkankampfflieg...

Phot. A. Müller,
Dresden-Los...witz

Unser erfolgreicher Kampfflieger
Leutnant Karl Bolle

657
...W.Sanke
BERLIN N 37...

Exzellenz von Hoeppner
kommandierender General der Luftstreitkräft...
und sein Generalstabs-Chef
Oberstlt. Thomsen

600
...W.Sanke
BERLIN N 37...

26e Citation à l'Ordre de l'Armée
DU CAPITAINE GUYNEMER (GEORGES)

Héros légendaire tombé en plein ciel de gloire, après trois ans
de lutte ardente ; restera le plus pur symbole des qualités de la
race : ténacité indomptable, énergie farouche, courage sublime.
Animé de la foi la plus inébranlable dans la Victoire, il lègue
au soldat français un souvenir impérissable qui exaltera l'esprit
de sacrifice et les plus nobles émulations.

Sold like postcards, the Sanke cards popularized the ace in Germany. Many Germans
collected the cards with the same fervor
as American baseball-card enthusiasts.

After his death in 1917 under mysterious
circumstances, French ace Georges
Guynemer was elevated by the popular
press to the status of a national martyr.

Allmenröder

Kampf-Flieger Nathanael

Fliegerleutnant Fahlbusch

sanitized the real work of the aces. Countering enemy observation aircraft and bombers was most often accomplished by killing their crews. The ace's work also reflected the attitude of the professional big-game hunter who stalks and kills his prey and brings home the trophy for all to see. Words coined to describe air combat imply hunting and killing. German air fighter units were called *jagdstaffeln*, "hunting squadrons," from the noun *Jagd* ("chase, hunt, pursuit"); the French derived the term *escadrille de chasse*, "pursuit squadron" from the verb *chasser* ("to go hunting"). As the words suggest, the more victories the ace scored, the more heroic he became in the eyes of his fellow countrymen.

An ace who had been a national hero while alive became a tragic hero after his death. An illustration of Georges Guynemer, one of the most famous French fighter aces, painted by René Lelong for a book titled *Un Héros de France, Guynemer*, depicted the young man being carried into heaven. The inscription described Guynemer as "the purest symbol of the race," hailed his "indomitable tenacity…savage energy…and sublime courage," and concluded that he would be "an undying memory which will exalt the spirit of sacrifice and the most noble emulations."

A closer look at Guynemer tells a story that in part contradicts these noble sentiments. In his physical appearance, Guynemer did not fit the popularized image of the fighter ace. A thin, intense, sickly young man who was pampered by his mother and two sisters, Guynemer, however, quickly established a reputation as the most reckless and feared of all French fighter pilots. He killed his foes at close quarters and gave every indication that he enjoyed doing it. Obsessed with improving his score, he sometimes flew five

This medallion, produced by the German government, commemorates Oswald Boelcke's death on October 28, 1916. The other side of the medallion shows a fanciful aerial scene and is inscribed with the words *"Kampf in den Luften"* ("Struggle in the Skies").

The Aerial Strategist

Before his death in 1916, Boelcke shot down forty enemy aircraft, won his country's highest military decoration, and received enormous popular acclaim. His most significant contribution to aviation, however, was as a combat flying instructor and aerial tactician.

Ordered to form a new kind of squadron specializing in aerial combat, Boelcke took an innovative approach. Unlike previous squadron commanders, who took little part in selecting flyers, Boelcke personally picked men who he believed had the potential to be successful fighter pilots.

Boelcke's method for developing his students' fighting skills was also innovative. Previously, German flight training only taught men to fly, but Boelcke taught them the art of aerial fighting. He took an active role in pilot instruction, flying in formation with new pilots and evaluating their performance. Boelcke also analyzed his own combat experience and wrote the first rules (dicta) for aerial fighting. Boelcke's dicta included advice that pilots be decisive, fire a well-aimed burst of fire from close range, keep their eyes on the enemy, and attack in packs of four or six. These simple lessons could be quickly understood, remembered, and easily applied by new fighter pilots. His pioneering work in tactics and organization has shaped the nature of aerial combat to this day—a contribution that had far greater impact than his aerial victories.

The Lafayette Escadrille

Although the United States did not enter the war until 1917, many Americans volunteered their services to the Allied military forces. Americans fought as volunteers in all branches of the British and Canadian military forces and served as members of the American Field Service, where they primarily drove ambulances. A few joined

sorties a day and on his best days scored multiple victories. He recorded his mounting list of victories with the precision of a big-game hunter.

In Germany, government and public adulation of the ace was no less than that observed in France. Oswald Boelcke's funeral was attended by the German crown prince, and his coffin was decorated with a floral tribute from Kaiser Wilhelm II himself. On October 28, 1916, the day of his death, Germans observed Boelcke Tag (Boelcke Day), in honor of the loss of their national hero. By royal decree, the Kaiser renamed Jasta 2, Boelcke's original squadron, Jasta Boelcke in his honor. Even his enemies recognized him. A British aircraft dropped a laurel wreath at the burial site with the inscription, "To the memory of Captain Boelcke, our brave and chivalrous foe. From the British Royal Flying Corps."

the Lafayette Escadrille, an elite group of Americans who flew for France.

In 1914 Norman Prince, a wealthy American aviator and founder of the Escadrille, offered his service to the French government in hopes of forming an American flying squadron. Drawing on the sizable ranks of Americans serving with the French Foreign Legion, Prince found six volunteers. Not only were these men adventuresome but they were also eager to leave the trenches, enter the prestigious flying ranks, and earn more pay. Both the high skill level of its pilots and its small size made the squadron prominent. Only seven men formed the original Escadrille. The group never exceeded twenty members, although many have claimed to have belonged.

Capt. Oswald Boelcke congratulates his fellow fighter pilots, with whom he worked in close conjunction. Flying together in Lille, France, Max Immelmann and Oswald Boelcke developed a team approach to aerial fighting. One pilot took responsibilty for attacking the enemy while the other, the wingman, flew behind and protected him from enemy attack. Because both pilots were flying fighter aircraft, they could easily switch positions in this two-man formation. Their approach was so successful that it is still used today.

III Ground to Air

"The pilot, viewing the progress of the war on earth from his airy eminence...remained aloft, aloof, lending himself to an event in which he could never really participate."

CECIL LEWIS, PILOT, ROYAL FLYING CORPS

WORLD WAR I (1914–1918) CAUSED

unprecedented destruction and loss of human life. The conflict began during the summer of 1914 as a localized confrontation between the Austro-Hungarian Empire and Serbia, and escalated into a global war between the Central Powers—Germany, the Austro-Hungarian Empire, and Turkey—and the Allies—France, Great Britain, and Russia. From 1915 to 1916, the war escalated to include Bulgaria, Romania, Greece, Portugal, and Italy. The United States, which had declined to enter the conflict for three years, was finally drawn into the war on the Allied side in 1917. By the war's end in November 1918, more than 11 million people had died and the world's political, social, and economic structures had forever changed.

For information about the Smithsonian's Fokker D.VII (pictured above), see page 103.

A Bolshevik party rally in Petrograd, Russia, 1917. After the fall of Tsar Nicholas II in March 1917, the Provisional Government elected to continue the war. Although this policy pleased the Allies, it proved to be the Russian government's undoing. Exploiting the war-weariness of the Russian people, the Bolsheviks seized power within eight months.

The defeat of the Turkish Army, which had enforced Turkey's rule over much of the Middle East, signaled the end of the 600-year-old Ottoman Empire. The victorious British and French arbitrarily redrew the region's map to include the states of Palestine, Transjordan, Syria, Iraq, Saudi Arabia, and the Persian Gulf Emirates. Disputes over the national borders set down by the Allies continue to this day.

Of the 65 million men mobilized by the Allies and Central Powers, more than 11 million were killed, and more than 21 million were wounded. If a monument similar to the Vietnam Veterans Memorial in Washington, D.C., were built to honor those killed in World War I, it would be more than eight miles long. Although casualties in the air war were overshadowed by the numbers of men killed on the ground, as many as 50,000 airmen were killed in World War I.

In 1917 Paul Nash, a soldier-artist, described the nature of the trenches, "The rain drives on, the stinking mud becomes evilly yellow, the shell-holes fill up with green-white water, the roads and tracks are covered in inches of slime, the black dying trees ooze and sweat and the shells never cease. They alone plunge overhead, tearing away the rotting tree stumps...annihilating, maiming, maddening, they plunge into the grave which is this land; one huge grave, and cast upon it the poor dead. It is unspeakable, godless, hopeless."

At the beginning of World War I, military leaders failed to foresee the changes that twentieth-century technology would bring to warfare. Many cavalrymen rode into battle clad in armor and wearing uniforms little changed since the early nineteenth century. This 1914 French cavalry *cuirass* (body armor) is based on a fourteenth-century design. It provided its wearer with little protection against machine gun bullets and shell fragments.

By 1915 the airplane, which could fly above the hazards of the battlefield, had largely replaced the horse-mounted cavalry as the primary means of observing the movement of enemy troops on the Western Front.

Within months of its beginning, the war seemed to move beyond human control. Governments could neither end the fighting nor control its spread across much of the globe. By 1915 war had spread throughout the world. On the Eastern Front, stretching from the Baltic to the Black Sea, the Tsar's army lost millions of men while attempting to protect the vast Russian frontier. In East Africa, a small band of Germans and colonial troops eluded capture throughout the war. French and British expeditionary forces supplemented by colonials from their empires fought desperate battles against the Turks in the Middle East. Austro-Hungarian armies exhausted their empire's resources while fighting Italy, Serbia, Romania, and Imperial Russia. But the trench war of the Western Front in Belgium and France, where the cost in human lives was highest, epitomized the tragedy of World War I.

From 1914 to 1918 Allied and German armies on the Western Front were locked in a stalemated war amid an impenetrable labyrinth of supply, communication, and attack trenches. Whether assaulting enemy positions or crouching in underground shelters, soldiers found little protection from poison gas, constant artillery bombardment, and deadly machine-gun fire.

In this setting of unparalleled horror, only fliers seemed capable of moving where they wished—free from the mud, barbed wire, and anonymous mass death of the trench war. Popular writers seized on this perception and portrayed World War I aviation as a romantic adventure. Contrary to popular belief, however, the airplane's impact on the war was limited. For four years, the focus of the war was not in the air but in the trenches of the Western Front.

Ground to Air: Learning to Use the Airplane

Interwar popular literature, including pilot memoirs, presented an image of the first air war that was almost totally disassociated from the rest of the war. Although appealing, this portrayal provides an oversimplified view of a complex historical event. A more careful examination of aviation's wartime experience reveals that the development of military aviation during World War I was intimately linked to the war on the ground. World War I had a far greater effect on the pace and direction of military aviation's development than aviation had in determining the outcome of the war.

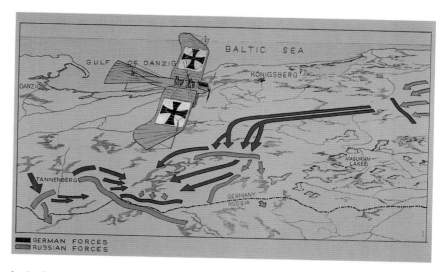

At the Battle of Tannenberg, the airplane helped the Germans win a spectacular victory with an army smaller than the attacking Russian forces. Flying over areas too large to be effectively reconnoitered by cavalry, German aviators tracked the advance of two Russian armies into East Prussia during August 1914. This information allowed German troops to surround the Russians.

The ability to take information gathered by fliers and disseminate it rapidly and accurately was one of the most important factors contributing to the German victory at Tannenberg. When German aviators returned from their reconnaissance missions, telephone operators (Fernsprecher) relayed the fliers' reports about Russian troop strength and positions to commanders on the ground.

During the first week of September 1914, Allied (French, British, Belgian) and German troops fought a decisive battle near the Marne River. Having sent some of its troops to the Eastern Front to fight the Russians, the German high command was left with a weakened army in the West. Instead of surrounding Paris as originally planned, German soldiers and cavalrymen attacked the city from the east.

French airmen noted the changing direction of the German forces in time for a reserve French army to mobilize in Paris and meet the German advance. The fresh French troops halted the Germans, who were exhausted from a month of marching and fighting.

French aviators, scrawling their observations on note pads, recorded the advance of the German army near Paris during the first week of September 1914.

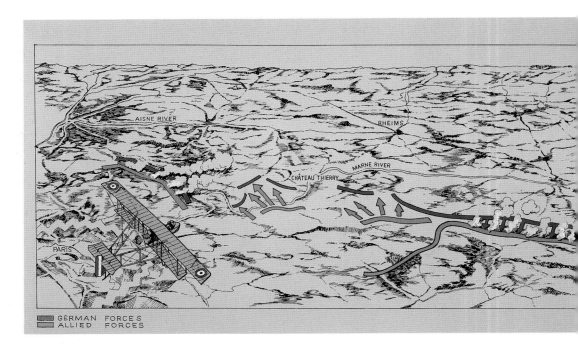

GERMAN FORCES
ALLIED FORCES

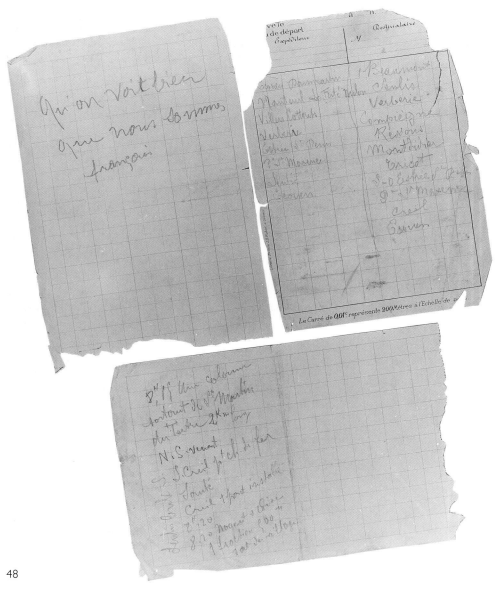

This model of the Jeannin Stahltaube shows that the aircraft carried no mounted armament. The Stahltaube was typical of the combat aircraft used during the first months of the war. Military leaders expected to use aircraft only to augment the cavalry's reconnaissance role and therefore did not consider armament necessary. However, some aviators carried pistols, and others dropped *fléchettes*, or aerial darts, on the enemy.

At the outbreak of hostilities it was not at all clear whether the airplane would play a significant military role during conflict. Although most of the military leaders of the major powers had predicted the value of aerial observation before 1914, the airplane was not a vital element in their strategic planning. The decisive role played by aircraft in the early battles of the war astonished commanders and convinced them of the potential impact of this new weapon on the ground conflict.

Despite the attempts of military leaders to integrate the airplane into their war strategies, military aviation played little part in shaping the course of World War I. The war, however, played a pivotal role in defining the tactics and technology of military aviation. During the key battles of the Marne, Tannenberg, Verdun, Somme, and especially Germany's spring offensives of 1918, the warring nations came to appreciate the capabilities and limitations of airpower.

Opening Moves of the War

During the battles of Tannenberg (August 26–31, 1914) and the Marne (September 5–10, 1914), ground commanders arbitrarily used aircraft to supplement the cavalry's observation role. While machine-gun fire and massed artillery could stop the cavalry, few antiaircraft defenses threatened airborne observers. An aerial observer could also cover more territory, move faster, and had a better view than a scout on horseback. As a result, aircraft played an unexpected and major role in these early battles. Aviation's decisive contribution proved its merit and promise, compelling the combatants to develop better defenses against aerial observation and to incorporate aircraft in their strategies.

As early as 1904 German war plans called for their armies to quickly encircle Paris to defeat the French before turning east to fight the Russians. This prewar strategy failed. When German troops confidently moved west in 1914, the Russians advanced unexpectedly and quickly into East Prussia. Reports made by aerial observers alerted the surprised Germans about their enemy's moves in the east. To counter the Russian advance, the German high command diverted some of its troops from France to strengthen its army on the Eastern Front. This strategy allowed the Germans to defeat the Russians at the Battle of Tannenberg. Mean-

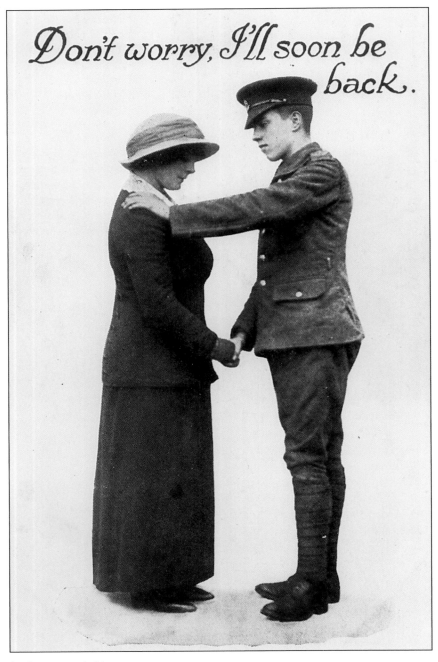

Don't worry, I'll soon be back.

As the war settled into a bloody stalemate, hopes like those expressed on this British postcard of August 1914 that soldiers would "soon be back" quickly faded.

while, on the Western Front, the diminished German forces turned to the east of Paris.

When German military leaders altered their strategy, they failed to appreciate that enemy aerial observation posed a menacing threat to its success. On September 3, 1914, French observation aircraft spotted the turning column of German soldiers and alerted the French army. French troops were mobilized as quickly as possible to halt the advancing Germans, and they met them on the banks of the river Marne.

The Western Front, 1915

At Tannenberg and the Marne, the airplane played a decisive role. Aircraft did not prevent the stalemate that followed the battles when, for instance, after their defeat at the Marne, the German army, unable to advance, began to dig in. The Allies, who found it impossible to advance through or around the German positions, also began to build permanent trenches. Within a matter of weeks, the combatants extended their trenches, forming an impenetrable line of fortifications, barbed wire, and machine-gun nests. By the spring of 1915, a complex trench system stretched more than 600 kilometers (400 miles) from Ypres, Belgium, to the Swiss border.

Attempts to break through the line only resulted in a disheartening cycle of gains and losses of ground. High casualty rates were unprecedented and astonishing—France lost 300,000 men in the first month of the war. The lines remained virtually static for the next four years. During the autumn of 1914, the expanding trench lines on the Western Front shattered Europe's hope that the war would be over quickly. In desperation, military leaders began to consider new methods and weapons, including the airplane, to break the stalemate.

Verdun: February–December 1916

During the Battle of Verdun, the airplane figured prominently in the German scheme to end the stalemate on the Western Front and in the French plans for defense. German aerial tactics reflected the novelty of coordinating air and ground operations.

Believing they could observe enemy positions and defend their air space without sending aircraft deep behind enemy lines, German military leaders launched an aerial blockade, or *Luftsperre*. Their airplanes flew up and down the

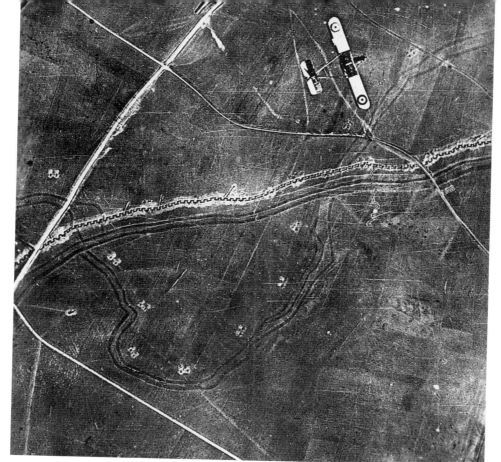

By the spring of 1915, a complex trench system stretched more than 600 kilometers (400 miles) from Ypres, Belgium, to the Swiss border.

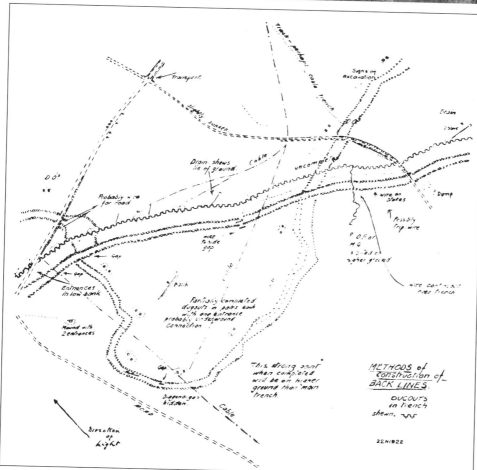

Diagrams drawn from aerial photos allowed army commanders to note such features as newly constructed trenches and roads, which often signaled an impending enemy offensive.

Pilots recognized that the most efficient way to aim machine-gun fire was to mount the weapon so that it fired directly along their line of sight. But this method of mounting remained impractical until a safe means of shooting through the propeller blades was found. The Fokker synchronizer solved the problem. Timing the machine gun to fire only when its bullets could not hit the propeller prevented damage to the propeller's blades and injury to the pilot from deflected bullets.

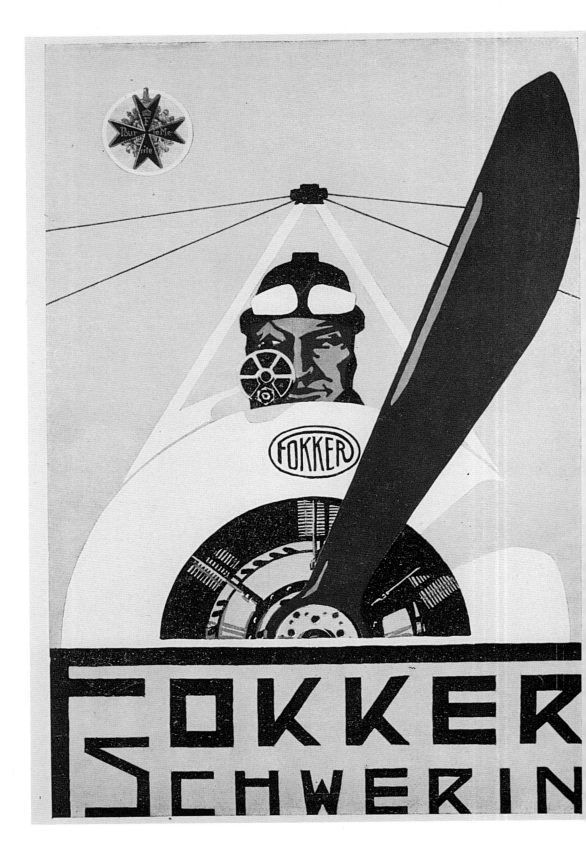

SUPPORT FIXE S M 50

POUR

FUSIL-MITRAILLEUR LEWIS

SUR NIEUPORT MONOPLACE

(TIR AU-DESSUS DU PLAN)

Ce dispositif est destiné aux avions Nieuport munis d'une mitrailleuse Vickers tirant à travers l'hélice.

Le support arrière possède un dispositif de réglage destiné à amener la ligne de tir du fusil-mitrailleur Lewis parallèle à celle de la mitrailleuse Vickers.

Ce support arrière n'est pas articulé, le réapprovisionnement de l'arme en vol n'étant pas prévu dans ce cas.

Les deux supports de l'arme sont en tôle et de forme fuselée. Le réglage arrière s'obtient simplement et exactement par un système de vis à pas contraires.

Le décliquetage du canon est commandé, par un câble et un anneau A.

La commande à distance de détente est obtenue par le dispositif spécial avec poignée du type A, montée sur le manche à balai (voir N° du catalogue 211.150).

Poids total avec collier Lewis : 5 k. 120.

Mounting a single Lewis machine gun on the wing of the Nieuport XI allowed the pilot to fire the gun over the propeller but made it difficult to clear a jammed gun or to reload.

To instill *esprit de corps*, each squadron chose a unique emblem, which they painted on the sides of their airplanes. Escadrille Nieuport No. 3, one of the first and most-effective squadrons, adopted the emblem of the *cigogne* (stork). Widely recognized in Europe as a symbol of good luck, the cigogne is also the symbol of the territory of Alsace, which France hoped to recover from Germany after the war.

front lines, attacking any Allied aircraft attempting to fly over German-occupied territory. From their vantage point over their own lines, German observers in airplanes and balloons could also direct artillery fire against the French army.

Central to the Germans' plan was the Fokker E.III. Although it differed only little from prewar designs, it had one major advantage: in early 1916 it was the only airplane that carried machine guns synchronized to fire through the propeller. Hoping that the E.III would easily fend off less well-armed Allied aircraft, the Germans relied on it, in combination with observation balloons to patrol the front trenches.

In contrast to the defensive aerial tactics used by the Germans, the French devised an aggressive offensive aerial strategy. By combining squadrons, or *escadrilles*, under one commander, the French were able to organize and coordinate attacks over the German front lines. In addition to developing tactics, the French also modified their aircraft in response to lessons learned from aerial fighting during the first year of the war. Lacking a suitable aircraft machine gun and synchronizer at the end of 1915, the Allies transformed single-seat scouting aircraft, such as the Nieuport XI, into fighters by mounting a single Lewis machine gun on their upper wings.

Innovative placement of existing armament gave the Nieuport firepower matching that of the German Fokker fighters. To turn the Fokker E.III, the pilot had to twist the airplane's entire wing surface. In contrast, the Nieuport pilot only had to operate the small, movable flaps (called ailerons) on each wing. The Nieuport's control system was more compact and efficient, and the aircraft was thus sturdier, easier to fly, and more maneuverable. Its lower wing was smaller than those of other contemporary biplanes. This sesquiplane (one-and-a-half wing) arrangement reduced drag, simplified maintenance, and increased the airplane's performance.

ESCADRILLE SPAD INSIGNIA

SPA 3

The Nieuport XI replaced the outmoded system of wing-warping with more compact and efficient ailerons. These small movable surfaces, situated along the trailing edge of the Nieuport's upper wing, allowed the pilot to bank and turn his aircraft more quickly than his German adversaries, who flew designs that used the older system.

The Nieuport XI played havoc with the enemy strategy. Germans quickly realized that they had too few aircraft to carry out their aerial blockade. Massed squadrons of French Nieuport XI fighters, which were superior to the German Fokker E.IIIs, penetrated German air space, shot down aircraft and observation balloons, and spotted troop movements.

By the end of the Verdun offensive, the Germans and French had both learned much about combined air-and-ground operations. Aircraft helped the French avoid defeat and thwarted German hopes of winning a quick victory. Neither combatant, however, had found a way to use aviation to end decisively the slaughter of trench warfare. The battle ended inconclusively in December 1916, with 542,000 French and 434,000 German casualties.

The Somme: July- November 1916

On July 1, 1916, the British army launched a major offensive north of the river Somme. The attack had two goals: to reduce German pressure on the French at Verdun and to break through the German lines, thus ending the stalemate on the Western Front and reestablishing a mobile war similar to the opening battles of 1914.

Aircraft played an integral part in the offensive. The British planned to send aircraft deep into enemy territory to spot targets for their artillery and to shoot down enemy aircraft. The scheme depended on reliable communication between the air and ground. When communication broke down, catastrophe resulted. Unable

Believing they could observe enemy positions and defend their air space without sending aircraft deep behind enemy lines, German military leaders launched an aerial blockade, or *Luftsperre*. Their airplanes flew up and down the front lines, attacking any Allied aircraft attempting to fly over German-occupied territory. From their vantage point over their own lines, German observers in airplanes and balloons could also direct artillery fire against the French army.

Once the Battle of Verdun began, German military leaders quickly realized that they had too few aircraft to carry out their aerial blockade. Massed squadrons of French Nieuport XI fighters, which were superior to the German Fokker E.IIIs, penetrated German air space, shot down aircraft, and spotted troop movements.

Spotting Artillery Targets

The British plan to break through the lines relied on clear communication between aerial observers, forward ground observers, and artillery batteries behind the front lines. A clock code—graphic, flexible, and almost impossible to misinterpret—was developed for the purpose. The aerial observer (see opposite top) considered the target to be the center of a clock. Twelve o'clock represented true north from the target, three o'clock represented due east, six o'clock due south, nine o'clock due west. If a shot landed due south of the target, the observer relayed that it had landed at six o'clock. Imaginary circles were drawn around the target to represent ranges of 10, 25, 50, 100, 200, 300, 400, and 500 yards. These ranges were identified by code letters: Y, Z, A, B, C, D, E, and F, respectively. Thus, the aerial observer flashed "C 3" in Morse code on a signal lamp to indicate that a shot had landed 200 yards east of the target.

The Aerial Camera

British military planners studied aerial photographs to identify potential targets for their artillery and to plan ground attacks. The British Mark I aerial camera (below right) was standard equipment for Royal Flying Corps observation aircraft in 1916.

The log entry of Lt. Cecil Lewis, 9 Squadron, Royal Flying Corps, best describes the limitations of the aerial observation camera at the time of the Battle of the Somme:

> It was slung on the side of the fuselage outside, and it was a real old studio model, complete with leather concertina, mahogany frame and boxes of plates... . There was a sort of rudimentary 'ring and ball' sight to give you some idea of what you were taking—as you leaned out into a 70-mph wind and tried to see through the sight without getting your goggles blown off. To take a photo you grabbed at a ring on the end of a bit of wire, which was skittering about in the gale, and to change the plates there was a sort of mahogany knife handle which you pushed steadily forward and then pulled back. This was at the back of the polished cigar box full of 24 plates.

Flare Gun

An aviator signaled that he had located a potential target for artillery shelling by shooting signal flares of various colors. Directed by the flares, ground observers who accompanied advancing infantry verified the target at closer range. The ground observer then fired a signal flare of a prearranged color to indicate that the aviator should direct the artillery's fire on the target.

Message Streamer

Directing artillery shells from his position thousands of feet above the ground and miles forward of the front lines, the aerial observer sometimes had to rely on the message streamer. After scribbling down his observations at the front, he secured the information in a pocket at the end of a lead-weighted streamer, returned to the British side of the lines, and dropped the streamer to the ground. A ground observer retrieved it and brought the message to the artillery batteries.

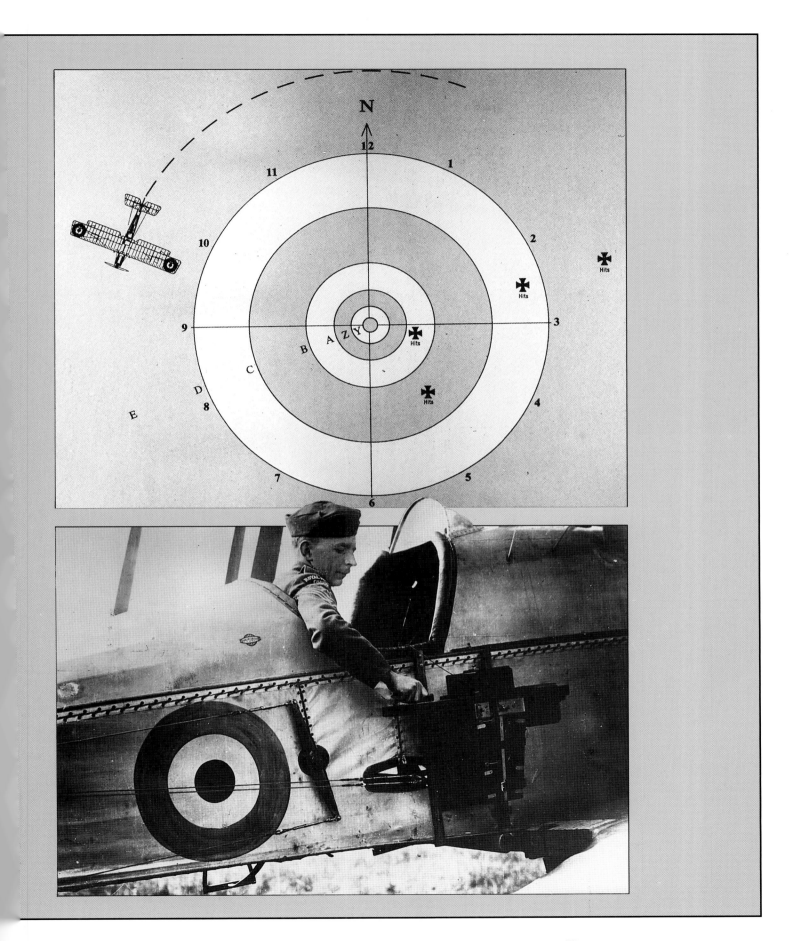

German generals inspect a Fokker E.III fighter, which they hoped would dominate the skies and ensure their success on the ground, before the Battle of Verdun.

The dislocation of civilians, destruction of property along the Western Front, and terrible casualties suffered by the French army in defense of its homeland plunged France into political, social, and economic disorder.

All warring nations relied on rigid and nonrigid aircraft to observe enemy troop movements and concentrations.

to coordinate aerial and ground operations to destroy the German defenses, the British army suffered a shocking defeat.

The British planned to use aircraft-directed artillery to devastate German defenses at the Somme. They assumed that a five-day artillery barrage would destroy German fortifications and the barbed wire that formed an impervious barrier between the Allied and German trenches. Once the artillery barrage had cleared the way, massed troops would walk across no-man's-land, oust the demoralized Germans from their positions, and allow the cavalry to break out into the open country behind the German lines.

The British plan began to unravel long before the first soldiers could advance from their trenches. The British high command failed to appreciate aviation's limitations when they planned their aerial strategy for the Somme offensive. The unwieldy system of communication between ground and air—a fundamental element of the British plan—broke down during the battle's first hours.

Aircraft and aerial cameras, on which British military leaders had depended in planning their offensive, proved inadequate. British aerial photographs could not show the depth and strength of the German dugouts behind the front lines or the German army's level of training and morale. In the safety of underground shelters, German defenders continued target practice and worked on drills to improve their speed in manning machine-gun posts.

Fog, rain, and the chaos of battle compounded problems caused by poorly designed aircraft and the complicated system of signaling between airmen and ground observers. Clouds of dust, smoke, and poison gas obscured British pilots' view of the battlefield and prevented them from seeing signal flares fired by artillery observers on the ground. The breakdown of communication prevented aviators from directing the artillery fire so vital to the success of the offensive.

The failure of aviation at the Somme led to carnage on the ground. The five-day, aircraft-directed artillery barrage did not cut the barbed

Just as tensions between professional soldiers and civilian draftees caused problems on the front lines, friction between the new members of the work force and trade unions sometimes disrupted production. In Britain, trade union opposition to the policy of hiring unskilled laborers was often hostile and sometimes violent. To maintain production, the British government had to put down strikes and promise male workers that their jobs would not be permanently filled by women. This female worker at a glass factory in Lancashire, circa 1916, would have no job security at the war's end.

World War I called for an all-out effort. The British high command summoned the help of every civilian and soldier, every man and woman. While the nation's men flocked to the recruiting offices, civilians on the home front streamed into the factories, where they helped to produce aircraft, artillery shells, guns, and ammunition for the war effort. For the first time, government labor policy allowed large numbers of women to enter jobs traditionally held by men.

THESE WOMEN ARE DOING THEIR BIT

LEARN TO MAKE MUNITIONS

wire, annihilate the German defenders, or destroy their fortifications. Expecting that aircraft-directed artillery fire had cleared their path, however, heavily loaded British soldiers advanced into no-man's-land. But the barbed wire that the barrage had not cut stopped them in their tracks. German machine gunners, whom the barrage had not killed, casually massacred them. By the end of the first day of the battle, the British army had suffered nearly 63,000 casualties.

The United States Enters the War

When the Somme Offensive was finally terminated in November 1916, the British Army had suffered more than 500,000 casualties without any appreciable military gain. As the deadlock on the Western Front continued into its third year, it had become clear to the political and military leadership of Britain and France that without direct American military involvement the Allies were unlikely to win the war. The administration of American President Woodrow Wilson, however, had maintained an official policy of neutrality since 1914, gambling that by supplying the allies with material and monies the U.S. would neither have to raise an army nor mobilize industry to equip it. By April 1917, convinced in part by the aftermath of the Somme Offensive, the man who had won reelection in 1916 with the slogan "He Kept Us Out of War," reversed his earlier policy and asked Congress to declare war on Germany and the other Central Powers.

The quick change in official policy left the armed forces unprepared, both on the ground and in the air. Never before called upon to fight a war of this geographical and technological scale, American military leaders also struggled to develop a strategy for using their air and ground forces to end the stalemate on the Western Front. Ironically, they benefited little from the European combatants' experience with using the airplane as a weapon and mobilizing the aviation industry.

Battle of Saint-Mihiel

Having consulted European military aviation planners, who now had three years of wartime experience, Gen. William "Billy" Mitchell, U.S. Chief of Air Staff, formulated the aerial strategy for the Saint-Mihiel offensive of September 1918. Mitchell

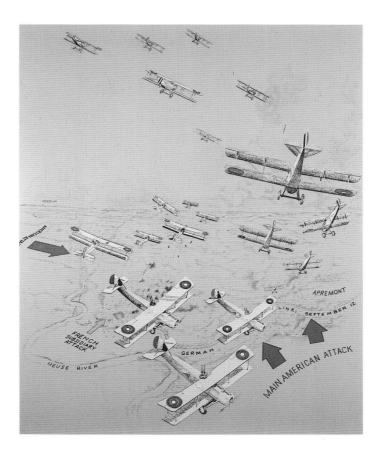

Commanding a massive force of nearly 1,500 British, French, and U.S. aircraft at Saint-Mihiel, Mitchell expected to overwhelm the German aerial and ground defenses from the sky. First, his fighters would free the skies of German aircraft and clear the way for artillery-directing observation craft. Once safe from the threat of German fighters, bombers would attack enemy supply depots and vehicles carrying materials to the front lines. Ironically, his plan was remarkably similar to the unsuccessful British aerial strategy during the Somme offensive of 1916.

In contrast to the U.S. Army Air Service's limited contribution to the war, U.S. Navy flyers performed a mission vital to the success of the Allied war effort. Long-range flying boats, such as the Curtiss HS-2L, escorted convoys of Allied supply ships, protecting them against attack by German submarines, seaplanes, and surface ships.

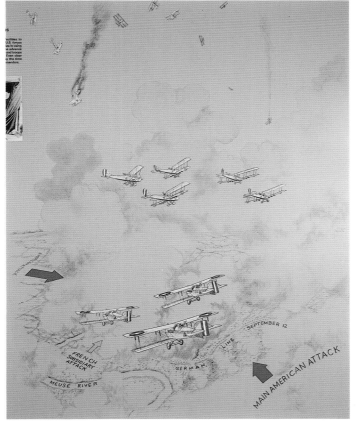

After a delay caused by poor weather, Mitchell's fighters succeeded in keeping most of the German aircraft away from the Saint-Mihiel battlefield. The reality of the battle, however, illustrated the deficiencies of Mitchell's attempt to combine new technology with old tactics. As in the Somme offensive of 1916, poor visibility and bad weather hampered the aviators' ability to support the ground attack. The offensive on the ground succeeded not because of the strength of Mitchell's air units, but because of the overwhelming numerical superiority of U.S. infantry.

PALS Battalions

An army of volunteers fought the Battle of the Somme. Rather than suffer the fate of an arbitrary assignment by an impersonal conscription agent, friends banded together to form what became known as PALS battalions. In Glasgow, Scotland, for example, tram workers formally joined as the 15th Highland Light Infantry. The few who survived after the battle, however, referred to themselves by their familiar name, the Glasgow Trams.

Although the PALS battalions' enthusiasm and numbers encouraged the nation, their inexperience did not inspire confidence in Fourth Army commander, Sir Henry Rawlinson. Having gained his military experience in colonial wars fought against natives by a professional army, Rawlinson was not convinced that the untrained, unprofessional PALS battalions would be able to follow anything but the simplest orders. The other commanders involved in planning the battle counseled Rawlinson to employ new tactics learned at Verdun. Rawlinson, because of his lack of faith in the PALS, dismissed their counsel.

At the heart of Rawlinson's plan was an aircraft-directed artillery barrage. The commander's expectations for observation aircraft did not take into consideration the individual craft's inherent faults or the general limitations of aerial observation. Even with state-of-the-art aircraft, the British could do nothing about the weather, which thwarted missions. When storm clouds or battlefield smoke obscured ground observers' signals from the aerial observers, they could do little to assist the troops on the ground.

Using prewar parade ground tactics, Rawlinson instructed the new army. Battalions were to advance in a series of waves, walking at a steady pace of less than two miles per hour and enter no-man's-land at one-minute intervals. They were to maintain their pace, even if they faced resistance, including machine-gun fire or uncut barbed wire.

Much to the dismay of Rawlinson's untrained troops, British artillery had neither destroyed the obstructive barbed wire nor the German infantry's firepower. Even though they realized that they faced imminent death, the PALS battalions obediently marched on. By the end of this first day, the 16th Highland Light Infantry Battalion (Glasgow Boys Brigade) had lost more than half of its ranks. This battalion's experience typified the fate of most of the British PALS.

Women filled positions made vacant when the "Glasgow Trams" did not return from battle. In many of the PALS battalions, three-quarters of the men died. These high casualty rates brought home the reality of the war. Bereaved communities, which had proudly sent their citizens to fight together, grieved that they had died together. After the Battle of the Somme, conscripts replaced the PALS.

"The companionship was marvelous, absolutely marvelous...We were all pals, we were happy, very happy together," Mason, a private in the British Army, later recalled.

In Glasgow, Scotland, a PALS battalion was raised over night. On the morning of September 13, 1915, James Dalrymple, manager of the city of Glasgow's Tramways Department, found that 1,100 of his employees had volunteered their services. Glasgow's response was typical of the camaraderie, patriotism, and faith in the glory of war that characterized all of the PALS battalions.

"I scrambled up the back of the trench, took up my position with my rifle on a small rise and opened fire blindly into the crowd of English soldiers who were coming across No Man's Land." Soldat Wilhelm Lange, 99th Reserve Regiment, German Army

The British attack came as no surprise to the men in the German trenches. Although the five-day artillery barrage had unnerved them, it did not stop them. They continued target practice and worked on drills to improve the speed with which they could man their machine-gun posts. They replaced the heavy (100 lb) mounts with small iron plates to ease carrying the weapons from the protective dugouts to firing stations in the trenches.

"The corps commander was extremely optimistic, telling everyone that the wire had been blown away, although we could see it standing strong and well, that there would be no German trenches and all we had to do was to walk to Serre." Brigade major of 31st division, British Army

"The behavior of the Highlanders seemed to us rather strange, for these came forward very slowly, either because of their heavy loads, or was it madness, without taking the least cover." German soldier, 170th Regiment

The overwhelming size of the U.S. ground force—as depicted in this photograph of American soldiers awaiting embarkation—was the key to the success of the Saint-Mihiel offensive. The U.S. Army Air Service was no more able to ensure victory by itself or prevent high casualties on the ground than its allies' air services had during earlier offensives.

expected aviation to play a critical role in reducing the bulge in the Allied lines near the town. Mitchell's lack of practical experience caused him to distort both the capabilities and limitations of the airplane. Although the Saint-Mihiel offensive on the ground was a success, aviation's performance did not measure up to expectations.

Commanding a massive force of nearly 1,500 British, French, and U.S. aircraft at Saint-Mihiel, Mitchell expected to overwhelm the German aerial and ground defenses from the sky. First, his superior numbers of fighters would destroy or chase away all German aircraft over the battlefront and clear the way for artillery-directing observation craft. Once safe from the threat of German fighters, bombers would attack enemy supply depots and vehicles carrying materials to the front lines.

Ironically, his plan was remarkably similar to the unsuccessful British aerial strategy during the Somme offensive of 1916. Like his European predecessors, Mitchell described his aviators as "independent cavalry." He based his tactics on the experience of mobile warfare, as used during the American Civil War (1861–1865), but with

the new technology of the airplane replacing the horse. Mitchell, however, failed to appreciate the inherent limitations of the aircraft with which he expected to implement his strategy.

After a delay caused by poor weather, Mitchell's fighters succeeded in keeping most of the German aircraft away from the Saint-Mihiel battlefield. The reality of the battle, however, illustrated the deficiencies of Mitchell's attempt to combine new technology with old tactics. As in the Somme offensive of 1916, poor visibility and bad weather hampered the aviators' ability to support the ground attack. The offensive on the ground succeeded not because of the strength of Mitchell's air units, but because of the overwhelming numerical superiority of U.S. ground forces.

German Offensives, Spring 1918

While the U.S. Army Air Service was just beginning to understand how to combine air and ground attacks, Germany had made great strides in aerial strategy during the first three years of the war. Attacking over the old Somme

In addition to carrying armament and ordnance adapted from ground weaponry, crewmen of German close-support aircraft were equipped with gas masks and steel helmets, exactly the same as those worn by ground troops. This equipment was essential for low-flying aviators when they attacked positions that were also being bombarded with high explosive and poison-gas artillery shells.

German aviators in low-flying, ground-attack aircraft used this makeshift aerial bomb against Allied soldiers in open trenches. The casualties and confusion caused by these attacks allowed German assault troops to bypass or destroy the Allied strongholds.

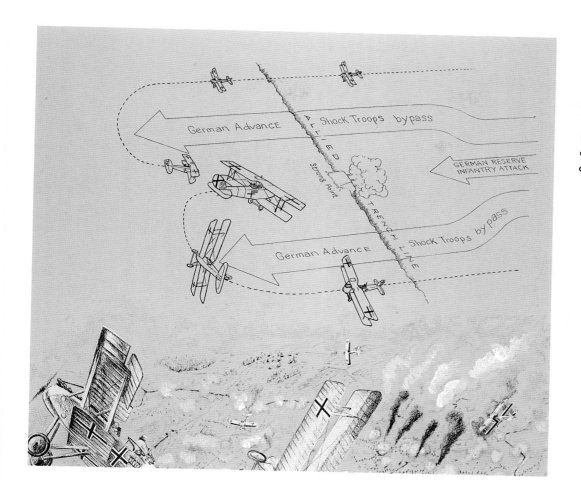

Within the illustration:

German Advance

Shock Troops bypass

ALLIED

Strong Point

GERMAN RESERVE INFANTRY ATTACK

TRENCH LINE

German Advance

Shock Troops bypass

Attacking first with the pilot's forward-firing machine gun, and then with bombs and the observer's rear-facing machine gun, the Halberstadt was so effective that the French proposed its surrender be required by the terms of the Armistice.

battlefield, Germany unleashed the *Kaiserschlacht* (later called the Ludendorff offensive by the Allies) on March 21, 1918. Instead of attacking in waves, as Allied infantry had done at the Somme, the Germans used many small groups of "shock troops" to infiltrate and bypass Allied positions under the cover of a barrage of smoke and gas shells. German reserve infantry units, assisted by ground-attack aircraft, then moved in to destroy the Allied positions.

The Halberstadt Cl.IV was one of the important weapons used during these last battles of the war. This lightweight aircraft combined the speed and handling of a single-seat fighter with the firepower and bomb-carrying capability of a

larger two-seater. Unlike other two-seat aircraft, the Halberstadt's distinctive communal cockpit placed the pilot and observer back-to-back to facilitate communication. These qualities made it an ideal aircraft for attacking enemy trenches in support of assault troops.

With the help of such aircraft as the Halberstadt Cl.IV, coordinated German air and ground attacks finally broke through the enemy lines, a goal that had eluded all the combatants. Because Germany had exhausted the last of its resources on the aviation build-up during 1917, however, its military forces were too weak to take advantage of their strategic success in 1918.

The Halberstadt Cl.IV carried a small but effective payload of grenades and mortar bombs. These small bombs were chosen to make the aircraft light and agile enough to avoid anti-aircraft fire at altitudes of less than 30 meters (100 feet) over enemy trenches. Because the intended targets of the German ground-attack flyers were soldiers in unprotected trenches, large bombs were not necessary.

The Voisin VIII:
Jack of All Trades

At the outbreak of the war, Voisin aircraft were among the few airplanes available for combat duty. During the first half of World War I, the French used Voisins to perform aerial observation missions. By 1916, they were being used to carry out night bombing missions over the Western Front, especially to bomb industrial areas in Germany. As newer planes designed specifically for these tasks were developed, Voisins were used for other purposes.

Because it provided a stable platform for observation, had a large carrying capacity, and was easily adaptable, the Voisin was used in all theaters of war, from the freezing Russian plains to the broiling Mesopotamian desert. For flying over the snow-covered expanse of central Russia, the Imperial Russian Air Service substituted skis for rubber wheels in landing gear. Equally adaptable to desert conditions, the sturdy Voisin VIII was used by the British Royal Flying Corps in the Middle East for observation, reconnaissance, and bombing.

Operating Voisin bombers provided the fledgling European air services with valuable experience at flying in harsh and diverse conditions around the world. As important as its versatility was its role as one of the world's

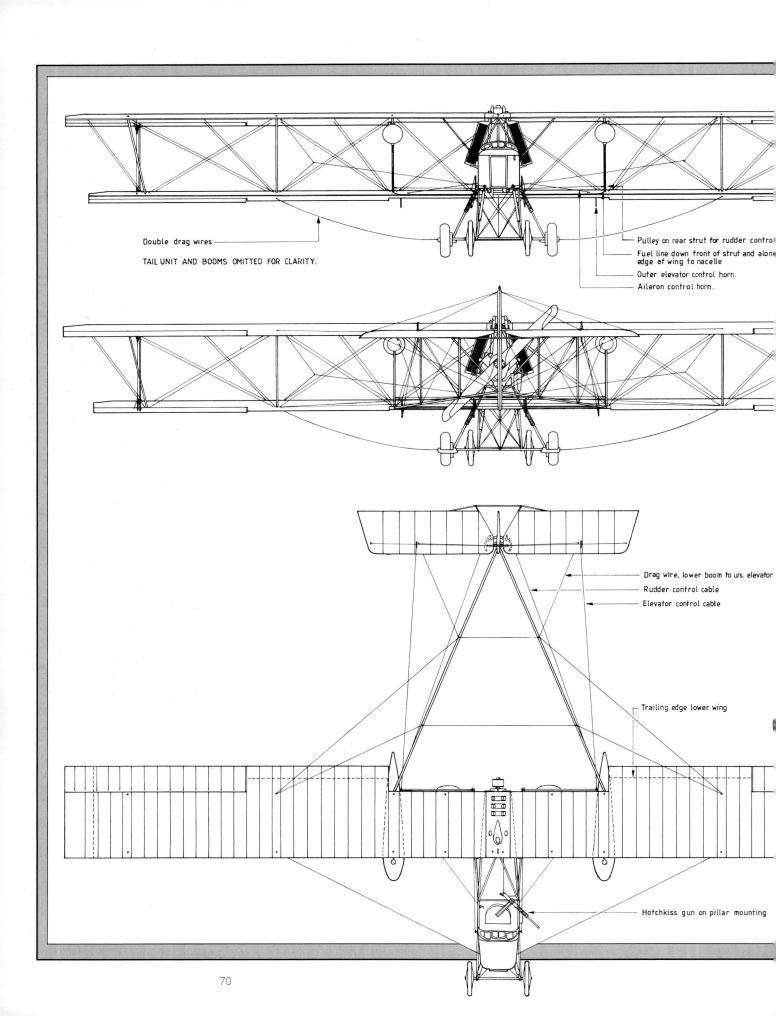

Double drag wires

TAIL UNIT AND BOOMS OMITTED FOR CLARITY.

Pulley on rear strut for rudder control

Fuel line down front of strut and along edge of wing to nacelle

Outer elevator control horn.

Aileron control horn.

Drag wire, lower boom to u/s. elevator

Rudder control cable

Elevator control cable

Trailing edge lower wing

Hotchkiss gun on pillar mounting

70

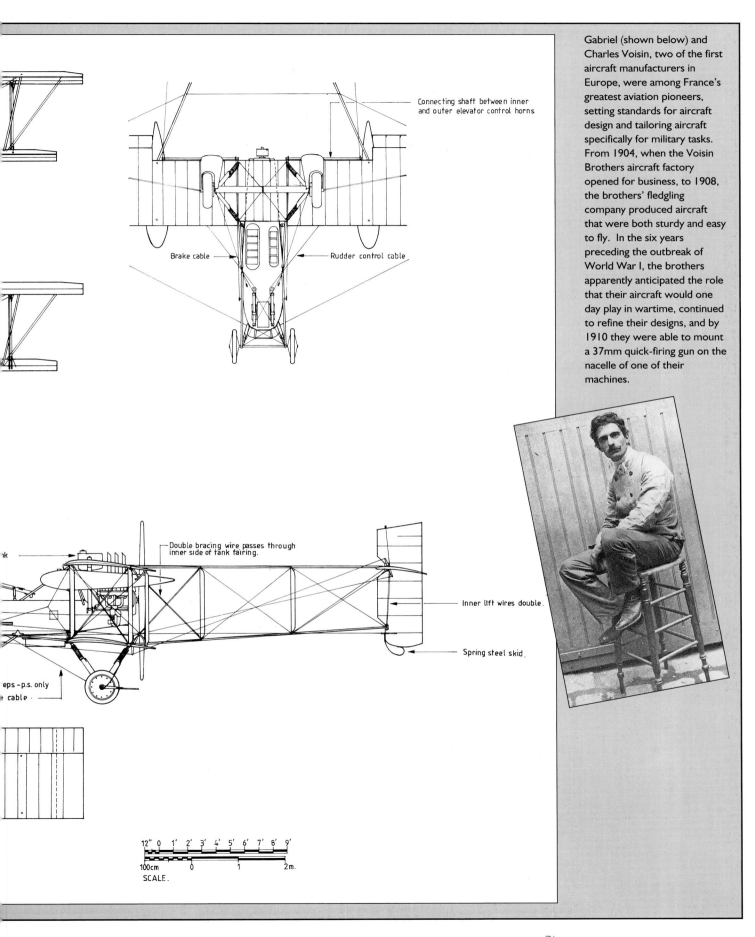

Connecting shaft between inner
and outer elevator control horns

Brake cable

Rudder control cable

Double bracing wire passes through
inner side of tank fairing.

Inner lift wires double.

Spring steel skid.

eps - p.s. only
cable

12" 0   1' 2' 3' 4' 5' 6' 7' 8' 9'

100cm   0   1   2 m.

SCALE.

Gabriel (shown below) and
Charles Voisin, two of the first
aircraft manufacturers in
Europe, were among France's
greatest aviation pioneers,
setting standards for aircraft
design and tailoring aircraft
specifically for military tasks.
From 1904, when the Voisin
Brothers aircraft factory
opened for business, to 1908,
the brothers' fledgling
company produced aircraft
that were both sturdy and easy
to fly. In the six years
preceding the outbreak of
World War I, the brothers
apparently anticipated the role
that their aircraft would one
day play in wartime, continued
to refine their designs, and by
1910 they were able to mount
a 37mm quick-firing gun on the
nacelle of one of their
machines.

OPPOSITE TOP:
The Smithsonian's Voisin VIII, circa 1918

OPPOSITE BELOW LEFT:
Pilot's seat and flight controls in the Voisin VIII.

OPPOSITE BELOW RIGHT:
After sixty years in storage, NASM's Voisin VIII waits to be restored.

first strategic bombers. From 1915 to 1917 Voisin VIII's carried out the first bombings of German towns and factories. Difficulties in finding their targets, aiming their bombs, and eluding German defenses rendered the French night bombers ineffective. But they remained a portent of things to come.

In the early part of 1917, the U.S. War Department Bureau of Military Aeronautics, purchased a Voisin Type VIII, which had been used in 1916 on the Western Front. As a representative state-of-the-art night bomber, the airplane was used to demonstrate the advances in aeronautics accomplished by the French. When the Voisin was reassembled and flown at the Aviation Experimental Station, Langley Field, in late 1917 and early 1918, however, it had already become obsolete. Rapid changes in aviation technology in France and other European countries had rendered the Voisin comparatively ungainly, slow, and poorly armed.

In July 1918 the War Department offered the obsolete airplane to the Smithsonian Institution for "exhibition purposes or historical record." The Smithsonian accepted the gift, and on September 16 and 17, 1918, six boxes and one crate containing three aircraft (a Farman and a Caudron had also been sent) were delivered to the National Museum.

When the crates were opened and inspected, it quickly became apparent that the Voisin was not complete. It

had been shipped without its engines or propellers. Apparently, the airplane's propeller was found during reassembly and, in October 1918, the Voisin, without its engine, was suspended from the ceiling of the South Hall of the Arts and Industries Building. In 1928 the Voisin VIII was removed from the exhibit hall, disassembled, and put in storage. In 1983, more than sixty-five years after it had been acquired, an engine was found for the Voisin VIII in the collection of the U.S. Air Force Museum in Dayton, Ohio. That engine was incorporated into the aircraft's subsequent restoration in 1989 for *Legend, Memory and the Great War in the Air.*

Perhaps the most innovative feature of the Voisin design was its internal bomb rack (left). At the beginning of World War I, bombs were dropped one by one over the side of the aircraft. The Voisin bombardier, by contrast, operated a handle inside the aircraft that allowed him to drop as many bombs at a time as he desired.

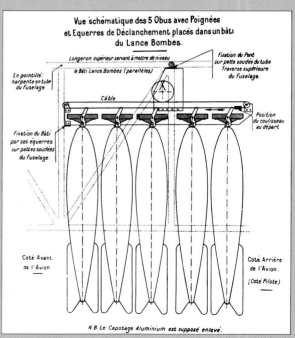

Vue schématique des 5 Obus avec Poignées et Equerres de Déclanchement placés dans un bâti du Lance Bombes.

IV A Hostile Environment

"I envied the flyers. Here was I in mud up to my knees either in the trenches or on the roads and getting very little out of war but lots of hard work. The other fellows were sailing around in the clean air while I had to duck shells all the time and run chances of being caught by the machine guns and snipers. Of course, the aviators were also being shelled, but they never seemed to get hurt."

E. M. ROBERTS, U.S. ARMY AIR SERVICE, PILOT AND FORMER INFANTRY-MAN, 1918

THE PERCEPTION OF THE AVIATOR'S life, expressed by E.M. Roberts, was commonly held by infantrymen. Contrary to the view from the trenches, however, wartime combat flying was every bit as hazardous as service on the ground. Although the number of aviators killed in combat during the war (about 10,000) amounted only to one-tenth of one percent of the approximately eleven million soldiers who died on the ground, flyers and infantrymen both faced about a 70 percent chance of injury or death during the war. With the odds of survival so low, the public adulation and official recognition afforded flyers did not always compensate them for the danger and stress of combat.

F.E.8

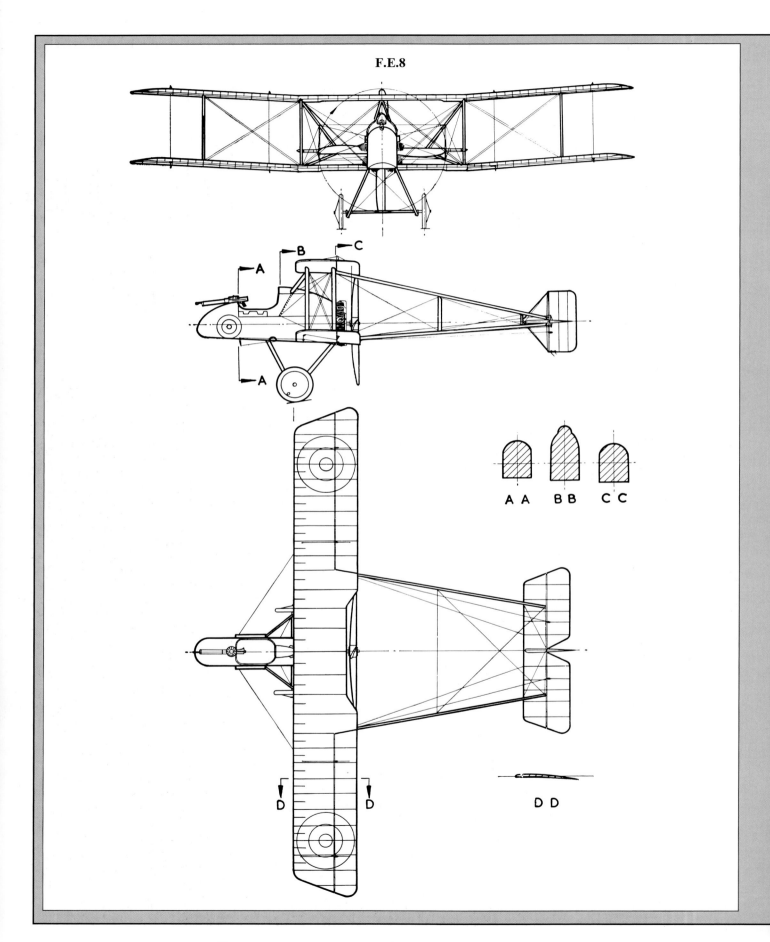

A A   B B   C C

D D

Royal Aircraft Factory Fighter Experiment #8 (F.E.8) Replica:
A World War I Rotary-Engine-Powered Aeroplane

Production delays on the home front often directly affected pilot safety at the battlefront, as the story of the British Fighter Experiment #8 (F.E.8) illustrates. In October 1915 the F.E.8 prototype was a state-of-the-art design. The Royal Flying Corps had great hopes for the innovative pusher (propeller mounted be–hind the wing) airplane, with its unobstructed field of vision and menacing Lewis machine gun mounted up front. Because the Royal Aircraft Factory was overcommitted at the time, it contracted the work on the F.E.8 to other factories, some of which had never produced aircraft.pThese inexperienced contractors slowed production. By the time the aircraft finally reached the front one year later, its performance had been surpassed by new enemy aircraft types. The F.E.8 was no longer a state-of-the-art fighter, but was an easy kill, a deathtrap for the men who had to fly it.

Royal Aircraft Factory F.E.8, circa 1917.

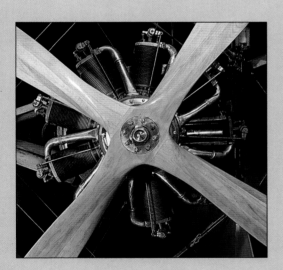

Le Rhône 9J Rotary Engine
The F.E.8's designers chose the French Le Rhône 9J rotary engine of 110 h.p. to power the aircraft. Among the best rotary engines of its day, the Le Rhône produced as much power as contemporary German inline engines at a fraction of the weight and allowed Allied fighters to be both fast and maneuverable.

For all its advantages, the rotary engine suffered from a number of inherent problems. The cylinders of a rotary engine spun around a stationary crankshaft, creating a powerful gyroscopic effect that resisted a pilot's attempts to turn the aircraft, often with fatal consequences at low altitude.

Like all rotary engines, the Le Rhône used castor oil as a lubricant. When the rotary engine was mounted in front of the cockpit, it sprayed the oil into the pilot's face, reducing visibility and causing unpleasant physical side effects, such as vomiting and diarrhea.

Lewis Machine Gun
Designers armed many of the first Allied fighters with the Lewis machine gun because it was the only efficient lightweight automatic weapon available. Unfortunately, its ammunition drum contained only forty-seven rounds and had to be changed frequently during combat, which was no easy task. The pilot had to let go of the airplane's controls, remove the empty drum, and replace it with a full one, while fighting the blast of the slipstream.

Student pilots in the British Royal Flying Corps learned about some of the hazards of combat flying from instructional diagrams and posters.

From their first training flights to flying in combat, aviators faced a hostile environment. Mediocre instruction during training cost many flyers their lives before they had even earned their pilot's certificate or qualification. Boredom at the aerodrome made pilots restless. As they waited for the next battle, there was time to think about squadron mates who had died and to wonder who would be next. Once in the air, they had to deal with equipment that was often poorly built or obsolete, making flying even more hazardous.

By the end of the war, some measures had been taken to improve aviators' chances of survival. Only the Germans, however, had the benefits of specialized flight clothing, oxygen equipment, and parachutes.

Training

"Fourteen hours! It's absolutely disgraceful to send pilots overseas with so little flying.... My God, it's murder."
CECIL LEWIS, ROYAL FLYING CORPS, 1916

Before the outbreak of the war, most military pilots learned to fly at civilian flight schools. As the air services of the warring powers expanded after the war had begun, the need for new pilots quickly overwhelmed the small pre-war training programs. In Britain, for example, the pilot-training program of the Royal Flying Corps lacked an adequate number of instructors and training fields. As a result, an estimated 60 percent of all British aircraft accidents occurred during training.

Yet, as combat losses of air crew increased, training of replacements was accelerated, further hindering the development of instruction programs. Many fledgling pilots had never even driven an automobile before they learned to fly. Instructional aids were primitive. Although placards and other on-ground techniques were used to explain how to perform various maneuvers or avoid enemy aircraft, nothing could replace actual flying experience. Aviators who survived flight training entered combat with as few as five hours of flying time. Poorly prepared to survive in

Flight schools in Britain improvised simulated cockpits mounted on rails to train pilots and gunners to compensate for aircraft movement when aiming at attacking enemy fighters. The effectiveness of the drill was never determined.

This photograph taken by a British aviator provides a somber reminder of the extraordinarily high loss rates experienced by some units.

the combat environment over the front, many flew into battle prone to making fatal errors.

Gunnery training was even more cursory than flight instruction. Many pilots received only one day of instruction before leaving for the front. Although pilots were expected to sharpen their marksmanship during their first few missions, many were killed before they ever fired their guns in combat.

By the war's end, each of the belligerents had sought to develop flight training programs that balanced the need to produce the large number of pilots necessary to replace losses at the front with the need to provide safe, competent instruction. In Britain, instructor pilots flew with their students, communicating via a tube connected to the student's helmet, an arrangement dubbed the Gosport system for the training field where it was invented. The system proved far superior to earlier methods involving hand signals. Because the Gospsort system was introduced at about the same time that British pilot losses at the front had reached critical levels, accelerated training pre-

vented many student pilots from receiving the full benefit of the new method.

The French system, in contrast, used no flying instructors. Student pilots began their training by taxiing a clipped-wing airplane called a "penguin," or *rolleur,* across the flying field. Although the penguin, like its namesake, was incapable of flight, it allowed new pilots to become familiar with an airplane's engine and flight controls before taking off for the first time in a flying trainer. Instructors monitored the student's progress and determined when he was ready for his first flight, which was performed alone. If he survived his first and subsequent flights in a slow, easy-to-handle trainer, the student pilot graduated to an operational training squadron, in which he would learn to fly a fighter, bomber, or observation aircraft.

Because its population was smaller than the combined total of the Allies, Germany possessed a smaller pool of potential pilots. To overcome this handicap, the German air service sought to reduce pilot casualties incurred during training as much as possible. Like the British, the Germans developed a pilot training program using instructors who flew with student pilots during the first phase of their training. In distinct contrast to Allied pilots, who often flew their first missions over the trenches with little or no knowledge of current combat conditions, new German pilots received instruction in the latest tactics at special training centers situated behind the front lines. Although these measures failed to counter Germany's numerical inferiority in pilots, they did increase pilot survival rates in training and during their first few combat flights.

Gray Hair at 22: Psychological Effects

"This flying job is rotten for one's nerves and although one is supposed to last six months with a fortnight's leave half way, quite a lot of peoples' nerves conk out after four and a half."

BRITISH WORLD WAR I PILOT

From the viewpoint of the soldier on the ground, the life of the pilot seemed easy. After a trip over the front lines, he left the war behind and returned to the relatively clean and warm aerodrome. There he drank, ate, played cards with his squadron mates, or worked on his aircraft while he waited for the next mission.

But beneath the seemingly easy life at the aerodrome lay the stress caused by the brutal reality of the combat flying. No amount of drink or diversion could disguise the turnover within the squadron or the feeling that death seemed almost inevitable. New faces replaced friends who had died in action, and before long many of the new faces had also disappeared. When a British pilot failed to return from a mission, his squadron mates said the pilot "went West," a nineteenth-century American expression for death that had crept into British usage during World War I. Facing the probability of a violent death, many aviators became superstitious. Some flew with into combat carrying good-luck charms, such as dolls or stuffed toys, hoping that these talismans would improve their chances of survival.

A Hazardous Profession

Flying itself was inherently dangerous. The aircraft of the period were physically exhausting to fly. Many types were powered by rotary engines that acted like gyroscopes, hinder-

Because military-issue flight clothing often proved inadequate, most aviators purchased their equipment from private suppliers before leaving for the front.

ing the pilot's ability to change the airplane's direction. Buffeted by winds as strong as 150 kilometers (100 miles) per hour, the pilot had to manipulate the levers regulating the air and gas mixture, the engine ignition-switch, the control stick, and the rudder pedals.

Poorly placed instruments added another degree of difficulty. To view the gas gauge on aircraft such as the British F.E.8 fighter, for example, the pilot had to turn around, taking his eyes off other instruments as well as enemy aircraft. Compasses and altimeters provided inaccurate information or, as a result of engine vibration, failed to function at all.

Controlling the gasoline and air mixture for the engine was perhaps the pilot's most demanding task while flying. To adjust the mixture, he had to take both hands off the control stick and operate the gas and air levers. To taxi or descend in an airplane powered by a rotary engine, it was more efficient to press the "blip switch," which momentarily cut the engine's ignition, than to fine-tune the air and gas mixture while trying to land. If a pilot held down the blip switch for too long, the engine's cylinders and cowling would fill with gasoline. When the engine was reignited, it would often catch fire or explode.

This photograph shows the oxygen system used by German pilots in the closing months of the war. Lack of cockpit space in the Fokker D.VII required that the oxygen container be mounted on the outside of the aircraft.

Equipping the Aviator

In addition to facing the hazards caused by unreliable aircraft, pilots flew into combat for most of the war with inadequate flight equipment. Early flight clothing consisted merely of a tight-fitting cap and driving duster with gloves. Such clothing offered little protection against the icy blast of the slipstream.

As aircraft performance increased, so did the need for better protective apparel. By 1914 aviators' goggles and protective helmets began to appear, but pilots continued to improvise their own flight clothing, often purchasing needed fur-lined apparel from private outfitters. Not until the need to clothe thousands of military aviators arose did the clothing industry begin to design and manufacture garments expressly for aviators.

As the altitude at which combat flights took place increased during the war, the corresponding increase in unexplained deaths among aviators led to the discovery of hypoxia—lack of oxygen because of high altitude—and forced the aviation industry to develop oxygen equipment. By the end of the war, experimental oxygen equipment allowed aviators to fly safely at altitudes greater than 3,050 meters (10,000 feet).

The liquid oxygen canister developed by Germany was the only successful oxygen system used in combat during the war. Oxygen flowed from a canister into a rubber bladder, from which it was hand-regulated, to a pipe stem held between the pilot's teeth. A nose clip prevented the pilot from breathing the thin air at high altitudes. Although primitive, this system proved quite effective and enabled German aviators to fly high-altitude photo-reconnaissance and bombing missions above the reach of Allied interceptors. German fighter pilots used the system during the final months of the war to climb to high altitudes, from which they could dive down and catch Allied aircraft by surprise.

Although the parachute existed before the beginning of the war, those produced by the Allies were too bulky to be worn by pilots or carried in the cockpit. Only Allied balloonists were equipped with these lifesaving devices. Germany and its allies, on the other hand, developed practical compact parachutes for their aviators by the spring of 1918. Despite occasional unreliability, parachutes saved many observation balloon crews and pilots from death by incineration.

Introduced in March 1918, the Heineke parachute was the first practical backpack parachute for aviators. Although German flyers were initially skeptical, by the final months of the war few entered combat without one.

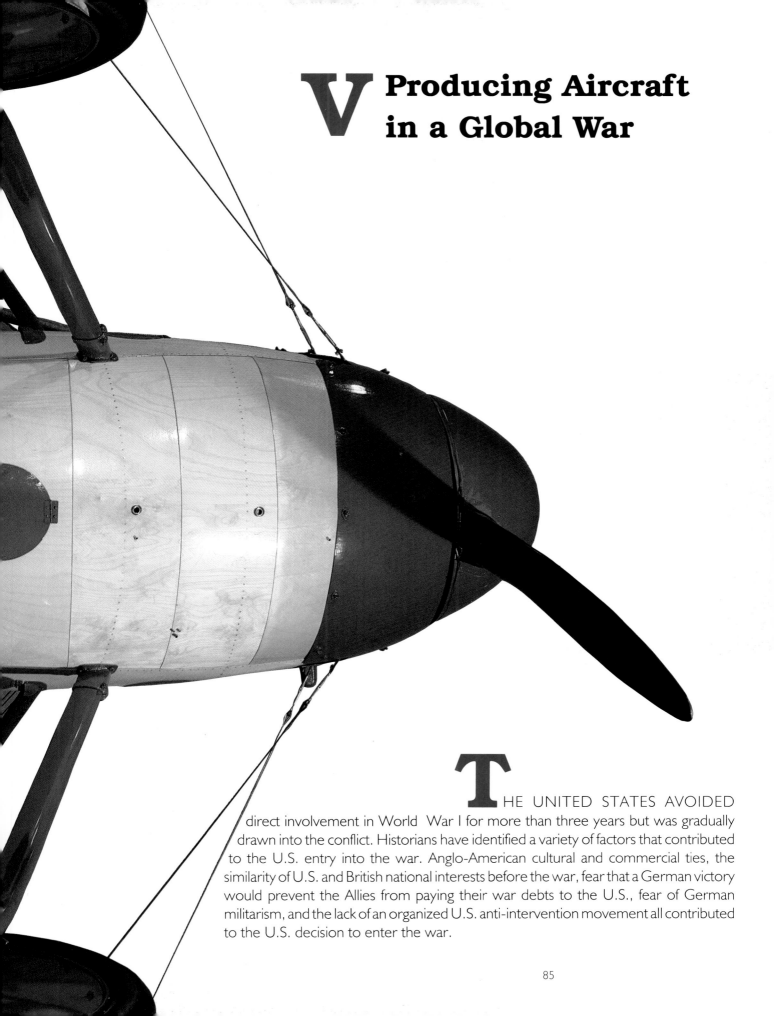

V Producing Aircraft in a Global War

THE UNITED STATES AVOIDED
direct involvement in World War I for more than three years but was gradually
drawn into the conflict. Historians have identified a variety of factors that contributed
to the U.S. entry into the war. Anglo-American cultural and commercial ties, the
similarity of U.S. and British national interests before the war, fear that a German victory
would prevent the Allies from paying their war debts to the U.S., fear of German
militarism, and the lack of an organized U.S. anti-intervention movement all contributed
to the U.S. decision to enter the war.

ALBATROS D-Va

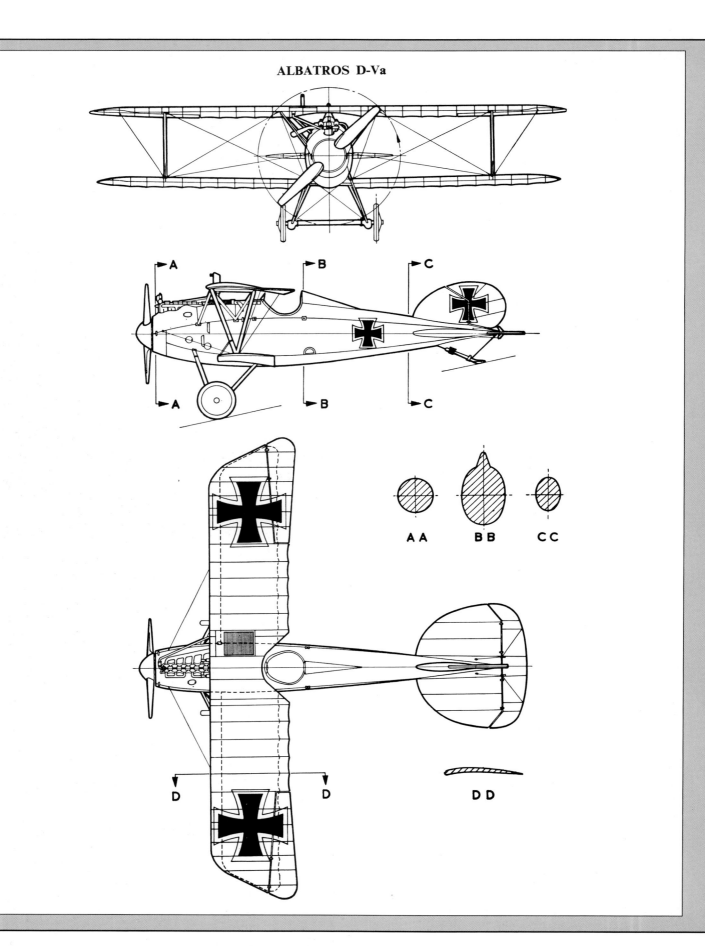

A A   B B   C C

D D

The Albatros Fighters:
Production versus Performance

The lineage of the Albatros fighters provides a vivid example of how aircraft were modified to meet new needs without slowing production. Before April 1917 designers modified the Albatros fighter primarily to improve its performance. But when the United States' entry into the war induced German industrial planners to maximize aircraft production under the scheme known as *Amerikaprogramm* (America Program), designers instead modified the aircraft to make it easier to produce. These final changes to the Albatros's design increased production rates, but degraded the aircraft's performance.

Wartime Experience: The Albatros D.I and D.II

Robustly constructed, fast, and well armed with two machine guns, the Albatros D.I and D.II of 1916 were among the first fighter aircraft designed with the benefit of wartime experience. Superior to contemporary Allied fighters, the Albatros D.I and D.II allowed the Germans to regain the advantage in fighter performance, which had been lost for most of 1916.

Building a Better Fighter: The Albatros D.III

When the Allies introduced the Nieuport XVII, which nearly matched the performance of the early Albatros fighters, German designer Robert Thelen was forced to refine the basic Albatros design to improve its performance. Thelen considered the French Nieuport's sesquiplane (one-and-a-half wing) V-strut configuration superior to the biplane layout of his earlier designs, because it had better downward visibility, was lighter, and had less drag. To save valuable time in development and prevent interruption of fighter production, Thelen simply copied the wing design of the French aircraft and incorporated it into the Albatros D.III.

Although the Albatros D.III's performance was markedly improved by the borrowed wing design, it also suffered from the same weaknesses that affected the French Nieuport. The single-spar lower wing flexed in flight, sometimes leading to wing failure in high-speed dives. The technology of the basic design had reached the limit of its potential. Further leaps in performance were impossible without a radical increase in power, reduction in weight, or improvement in streamlining.

The Last Gamble: The Albatros D.Va

"The D.V is so outdated that one does not risk anything with it. And the people at home, for nearly a year, have developed nothing better than the lousy Albatros."
MANFRED VON RICHTHOFEN, JULY 18, 1917

Much to the chagrin of the men who had to fly them in combat, the Albatros D.V and the similar D.Va could not compete on even terms with newer Allied fighters, such as the more powerful French SPAD XIII and British S.E.5a or the more maneuverable British Sopwith Camel.

The Albatros D.V and D.Va differed only in the arrangement of their aileron control cables. They both retained the single-spar lower wing and V-strut arrangement of the D.III, in spite of the lower wing's dangerous tendency to flex. Because the German aviation industry lacked the resources to maintain production rates and correct design flaws at the same time, it continued to produce the aircraft.

Because design defects were not corrected at the factory, maintenance crews had to modify brand-new aircraft before they could be flown safely. Ground crews added small auxiliary struts at the base of each wing strut on the Albatros D.V and D.Va to strengthen the connection and reduce the lower wing's tendency to twist. The problem was never entirely solved, and the corrective measures added weight to an already-obsolete design.

The Smithsonian's Albatros D.Va toured the United States as part of a war bond drive during 1918. The significance of the legend "Stropp" remains unknown.

Advertisements for the Albatros fighters, such as this one printed in a German aviation magazine during 1917, stressed the connection between the air war and ground war.

Propaganda posters, like this one by Carroll Kelly, expressed American expectations for military aviation in 1917.

FORWARD AMERICA !

On April 6, 1917, President Woodrow Wilson asked Congress to declare war on Germany and its allies. Amid an enormous outpouring of patriotic sentiment that followed, U.S. policymakers faced the daunting task of preparing America's undeveloped aviation industry and embryonic military air service to fight a modern war. The U.S. military and aviation industry, which for the first three years of the war had received little federal funding, suddenly received a huge infusion of money as Congress became convinced that the airplane represented the best way to become involved quickly and decisively in the war. Although such patriotic fervor characterized American planning and mobilizing, the country's leaders had little firsthand knowledge of the realities of the European war.

U.S. Aircraft Production: Death by Delay

"The road to Berlin lies through the air. The Eagle must end this war."

HOWARD E. COFFIN, CHAIRMAN OF THE AIRCRAFT PRODUCTION BOARD, JUNE 1917

When the United States entered the war, it possessed only fifty outdated military aircraft and had no plan for mobilizing and deploying

"We are coming, brothers, coming, A hundred thousand strong!"

"Voici la République sœur, Avec vous, frères d'armes, de cœur!"

In 1917 the U.S. aviation industry was unprepared. U.S. automobile and fledgling aviation industries, which profited from supplying the Allies with materiel, were reluctant to gear up before the U.S. officially entered the war.

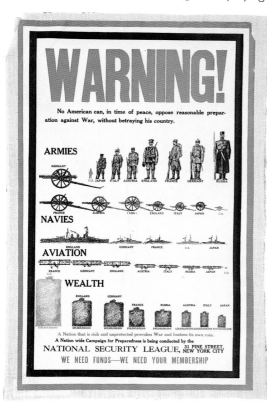

Transatlantic distance and wartime secrecy also thwarted the aviation industry's attempts to produce quickly state-of-the-art aircraft once the war began. Of the estimated 22,625 aircraft and 45,250 engines needed to meet U.S. and Allied requirements for 1918, only about 11,750 aircraft and 15,500 engines were produced.

The Buick Motor Company, which built the first 8-cylinder Liberty engine, and the Packard Motor Company were two of seven U.S. automobile manufacturers that received contracts to produce a total of 22,500 twelve-cylinder Liberty engines. None of these companies attained planned production levels before the end of the war.

the air service it expected to send overseas. Fully aware of the undeveloped state of the U.S. aviation industry, Congress appropriated huge increases in funding for aircraft production.

American planners hoped to apply the mass-production techniques pioneered in the automobile industry to the manufacturing of aircraft and aircraft engines. They enthusiastically expected that the United States could produce enough aircraft to supply not only its own needs but also those of its allies by 1918.

Wartime propaganda exaggerated the number of aircraft that the U.S. would produce—with estimates ranging up to one hundred thousand. Mass-produced aircraft, however, did not roll off the assembly lines. Instead, the United States struggled to produce only 1,200 combat aircraft before the end of the war.

Liberty Engine

American aviation companies built primarily British-designed airframes, but did produce the Liberty Engine. Civilian planners expected to produce a standard engine for use in all U.S.-built aircraft by adapting automotive tech-

nology and production methods. Pressure to begin production led to the design of the 8-cylinder Liberty engine in just six days.

Problems in adapting automobile engine technology to the needs of aviation delayed production long enough to make the initial Liberty engine obsolete. The failure of the 8-cylinder Liberty led to the design of a 12-cylinder model, further delaying large-scale production. By June 1918, the deadline for meeting the production goal of 4,500 engines, fewer than 1,300 Liberty engines had been produced.

The four additional cylinders made the Liberty engine heavier than many European engines of similar power. As a result, it could not be used in most of the European aircraft that were being considered for production in the United States.

Expectations for the "Liberty Plane"

Before entering the war, the U.S. aviation industry had produced only one suitable aircraft design—the Curtiss JN-4 "Jenny". Except for the "Jenny" and the Curtiss flying boats that

Text on aircraft in image: I AM SHIP Nº 1000 / WILL LEAVE FOR FRANCE JULY 31ST / 4:30 P.M. / 1000 HURRAH!!! / 1001 / THE DAYTON-WRIGHT AIRPLANE CO. / PLANT I - MOTOR TEST - JULY 29 - 18.

successfully patrolled the North Sea and English Channel, the United States relied primarily on European military aircraft. In July 1917 a Commission of U.S. Army officers under Raynal C. Bolling was dispatched to Europe to evaluate the air war and the aircraft types being produced by each of the Allied powers, to determine which were best suited for production in the United States. The Bolling Commission initially recommended that the United States concentrate on the production of Caproni heavy bombers, but the commander of the American Expeditionary Force in France, Major General John J. Pershing, overruled the commission on this point, citing the need for a variety of aircraft to be used in direct support of the army at the front.

As a result of Pershing's ruling, the commission recommended that the United States produce several types of military aircraft, including fighters and the British-designed DH-4 day bomber. The DH-4, which was the only American-built airplane to see action on the Western Front, was accepted for production primarily because it could use the Liberty engine.

American planners envisioned the DH-4 as the primary U.S. military aircraft. Initial, opti-mistic production estimates called for the manu-facture of 10,000 DH-4s. Manufacturing difficul-ties caused delays as soon as production began. The DH-4's plans called for the tolerances of all the aircraft's screws and bolts to comply with British standards, which were incompatible with U.S. standards. Once production began, work-ers found that the assembly-line method of auto-mobile production could not be easily adapted to aircraft manufacture. Some aircraft subassem-blies, such as the wings, fuselage, and engine, could be joined on an assembly line. However, other parts of the assembly process, such as covering the wings, applying dope (lacquer) to the fabric covering, and attaching the wire rigging, required skilled workmanship or were very time consuming.

By the end of the war, assembly-line tech-niques had been successfully applied to the pro-duction of the Liberty engine. Attempts to mass produce aircraft, such as the DH-4, however, failed miserably. Because of the delays encoun-tered in producing the aircraft, only a few U.S. squadrons were able to enter combat in France in 1918 equipped with DH-4s. Even though the DH-4, known as the "Liberty Plane," had satisfied

The DH-4 bomber was among the aircraft chosen for production in the United States, primarily because it could use the U.S.-built Lib-erty engine in place of the British-built Rolls Royce Eagle that powered British-produced DH-4s.

Mobilizing a Diverse Society

Propaganda played as important a role in mobilizing troops and raising the interest and eventually the morale of Americans as it had in Europe. Adding to the problems of the Committee on Public Information, established in 1917 to garner public support for the war, however, was America's striking social diversity. The United States entered the war following a period of intense social and political upheaval. The migration of African Americans from the rural South and waves of southern and eastern European immigrants had changed the population of northern industrial cities and the established political order. Some policymakers felt threatened by these changes and argued that ethnic diversity and class divisions would impede U.S. mobilization for war.

In reality, the enormous surge of patriotic sentiment that accompanied America's entry into the war cut across class, ethnic, and racial lines. Although World War I did not erase ethnic and racial divisions in American society, people from nearly every background joined in the war effort. Many Americans felt they could best serve the Allied cause by taking to the air.

African Americans volunteered for military service in great numbers, but were not allowed into the air service. Contrary to the imagery of recruiting propaganda, few black units saw combat with the American Expeditionary Force. While black soldiers fought under French command as infantrymen, the U.S. Army pressed African Americans into service as stevedores and laborers. Blacks were barred from the U.S. Marine Corps and the pilot section of the U.S. Army Air Service. Fighting for democratic principles while in a segregated military underscored the gulf between idealism and reality in American society.

Through an extraordinary combination of persistence, skill, and luck, one African American did become a combat pilot during World War I. After a lynch mob threatened to kill his father, Eugene Jacques Bullard fled from the United States to France in 1911. When the war began, he enlisted in the French Foreign Legion, then transferred to a regular French army infantry unit. Though he was wounded twice and declared disabled, he applied for pilot training with the French air service. Accepted on the basis of his combat heroism, he flew more than twenty combat missions.

Of the men who volunteered to fly for the Allies before the United States entered the war, a disproportionately large number came from elite northeastern colleges and universities. Following these other Ivy League students, Princeton University student George Vaughn volunteered for the U.S. Army Air Service in August 1917. As a member

of the Oxford Group, Vaughn learned to fly in Great Britain. He served with the British Royal Flying Corps on the Western Front from March to August 1918, then returned to the U.S. Army Air Service for the remainder of the war.

The son of Italian immigrants, Fiorello Henry La Guardia spent his early years in Arizona, New York City, and Europe. He paid his own way through law school and was elected to Congress in 1916. The following year he began to learn how to fly in a homebuilt airplane and then joined the U.S. Army Air Service. His aviation experience, political position, and ability to speak Italian prompted officers of the Air Service to appoint him as deputy commander of the American pilot training program at Foggia, Italy. Under his direction, 406 Americans completed training at Foggia. Most of the program's graduates, including La Guardia, served with the Royal Italian Air Service flying Caproni multiengined bombers on raids against Austria-Hungary.

1.

"Liberty And Freed
Shall Not Perish
A. Lincoln"

COLORED MEN
The First Americans
Who Planted
Our Flag
on the
Firing Line

TRUE SONS OF FREEDOM

2.

1. The names listed on the war loan poster reflected the ethnic diversity of the United States in 1917.

2. Contrary to the picture painted in propaganda posters, the United States military gave few African Americans the opportunity to fight in infantry units. None was allowed to pilot or maintain aircraft.

3. When the United States entered the war, the pilots of the Lafayette Flying Corps—600 Americans who served in various French combat squadrons—transferred to the U.S. Army Air Service. But because it barred black Americans from flying, the Army denied Eugene Jacques Bullard the opportunity to serve his country as a pilot.

4. Fiorella Henry La Guardia's (left) squadron flew its missions in Caproni bombers, built by Italian airplane designer and manufacturer, Gianni Caproni (right).

3.

4.

The *Lusitania* was the world's largest passenger ship in 1915. Onlookers would crowd the wharf when the well-known steamship embarked on trans-atlantic journeys.

In 1915, despite warnings from German diplomatic sources, the *Lusitania* set sail for Great Britain. Carrying British and American citizens as well as munitions for the Allies, the ocean liner was sunk by a German submarine off the coast of Ireland, resulting in the loss of nearly 1,200 men, women, and children, 128 of them Americans. The sinking of the *Lusitania* drew much notoriety, further heightened the tension between the United States and Germany, and nearly wrecked German-American diplomatic relations.

NOTICE!

TRAVELLERS intending to embark on the Atlantic voyage are reminded that a state of war exists between Germany and her allies and Great Britain and her allies; that the zone of war includes the waters adjacent to the British Isles; that, in accordance with formal notice given by the Imperial German Government, vessels flying the flag of Great Britain, or of any of her allies, are liable to destruction in those waters and that travellers sailing in the war zone on ships of Great Britain or her allies do so at their own risk.

IMPERIAL GERMAN EMBASSY
WASHINGTON, D. C., APRIL 22, 1915.

military requirements for an observation and bomber aircraft in 1917, it was dangerously obsolete by the time it entered combat.

Germany's Desperate Gambles

In 1917 the prospect of the U.S. joining with the Allied forces moved Germany to take desperate actions. Seriously weakened by the Allied naval blockade that had been in effect since the beginning of the war, Germany reinstituted its previously abandoned policy of unrestricted submarine warfare. In 1915 diplomatic relations between German and the U.S. were nearly severed after the *Lusitania*, a British passenger liner carrying a large number of Americans, was sunk by German submarine. Although they risked drawing the U.S. into the war on the Allied side if their plan failed, German military leaders believed that they could defeat their enemies by using submarines to destroy Allied supply routes.

The entry of the United States into the war

Throughout 1915 and 1916 German submarines (*U-Boote*) were instructed to attack only military ships and those flying the flag of Great Britain or its Allies. By the end of January 1917, German military leaders ordered the German navy, including seaplanes as well as submarines, to attack all ships supplying the Allies, even neutral ones, though they knew this action might bring the United States into the war. This blockade weakened the Allies, but ultimately the policy back-fired. The sinking of merchant ships and the accompanying deaths of U.S. citizens fueled war fever in America.

Desperate to introduce a more powerful replacement for the standard 160-horsepower Daimler-Benz Mercedes aircraft engine, but fearing that a slow-down in aircraft production would occur if time were taken to design and develop a radically different new powerplant, German engineers attempted to squeeze more power from the basic Mercedes engine. After his ideas for improving the engine were rejected, Daimler-Benz designer Max Friz left the company to start Bayrische Motoren Werke (BMW). There he designed an engine that retained the 6-cylinder inline configuration of the earlier Daimler-Benz engines but was superior in all respects.

Spurred by shortages of aircraft-quality wood and skilled labor, the Fokker Aircraft Company turned to using steel tubes in such aircraft as the Fokker D.VII. The need to use a careful welding technique and high-grade steel for airframes had initially prevented mass production of steel-framed aircraft. The Fokker company, however, discovered that readily available low-grade steel could be welded easily by unskilled workers.

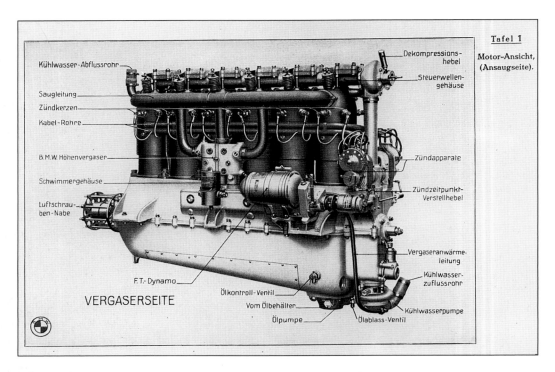

By 1917 rubber was scarce in Germany. The situation became so desperate that German women were encouraged to donate their hair, which could be used to reinforce rubber drive belts for industrial machinery needed to produce aircraft.

Every European power drafted soldiers from its colonies. In East Africa, Germany used African mechanics to maintain aircraft. Having aided the war effort, Africans and other colonial peoples increasingly sought independence from the Europeans.

in April 1917 also created a dilemma for German military and industrial planners. Increased output of fighter aircraft was obviously needed, but Germany lacked the resources to develop improved fighter aircraft and increase production at the same time. Gambling that the Albatros fighters' superiority over Allied types could be maintained, Germany industry increased production of the Albatros D.V. This policy was appropriately named the *Amerikaprogramm* (America Program).

Adopting this industrial strategy, which focused on producing the greatest quantity rather than on improving the quality of aircraft, was an act of desperation. Experience with producing aircraft engines had already taught the Germans the problems of standardization. The Daimler-Benz company's virtual monopoly on the production of aircraft engines in Germany stifled research and development for other engines. As a result, when the Allies introduced a new generation of high-performance engines in 1916, Germany found itself without a suitable replacement for its now-obsolete standard aircraft power

plant, the 160-horsepower Daimler-Benz Mercedes. When Daimler-Benz designer Max Friz proposed a new engine that used the same technology as the older Mercedes, but was more powerful, his ideas met with resistance.

The *Amerikaprogramm* stretched the German worker and aircraft industry to the limit. Germany was forced to take drastic measures to maintain production levels. Unskilled workers, many of them women and children, were bolstered by sailors from the German High Seas Fleet, many of whom were skilled machinists. These measures contributed laborers for production and freed additional manpower for the army.

By the end of 1917, Germany's *Amerikaprogramm* had clearly failed to produce aircraft capable of maintaining aerial dominance over the Western Front. Much to the chagrin of the men who had to fly it in combat, the Albatros D.V and similar D.Va could not overwhelm the more powerful SPAD XIII and S.E.5a or the more maneuverable Sopwith Camel, recently introduced by the Allies. German planners urgently

sought new aircraft to replace the Albatros fighters, despite potential interruption of aircraft production and lack of resources. Taking advantage of the end of the Albatros monopoly, such designers as Claudius Dornier and Hugo Junkers built prototypes of aircraft that they had designed earlier, but which had not received government support.

During 1918, at the test flying field at Adlershof, Germany, combat pilots evaluated and compared the performance of technologically advanced aircraft prototypes. Influenced by these tests but reluctant to embrace some of the radical new technology, German planners chose the Fokker D.VII and Pfalz D.XII, which incorporated only a few advanced features, for mass production in 1918. As the prospects for victory deteriorated during 1918, desperation overruled the conservatism of pilots and planners, who became more willing to consider innovative aircraft.

The Dornier Do.I and Junkers J.I incorporated metal into their designs. Dornier designs differed from conventional wood-and-fabric air-

craft, such as the American Curtiss JN-4D "Jenny." Rigging held together the intricate wooden internal structure of the Jenny's wings and fuselage. The fabric skin on the fuselage and wings provided some strength, but its major function was to provide lift, reduce drag, and protect the internal structure.

In contrast, the Dornier Do.I had a simpler internal structure and did not need rigging. A thin metal skin, riveted over a metal framework, not only held the airplane together but also provided the same functions as the Jenny's fabric covering. This metal "stressed-skin" construction greatly increased strength with little increase in weight.

Of all the metal aircraft tested in the final year of the war, the Junkers J.I was the only one to see combat service. Even conservative military planners accepted the value of using all-metal aircraft for attacking ground targets, because metal aircraft were more resistant to antiaircraft fire than conventional wood-and-fabric designs.

In addition to its all-metal construction, the J.I incorporated another advanced feature, the

Officials inspect the Dornier Do.I, one of the entries at the Adlershof fighter design competition, July 1918.

Like the Pfalz D.XII (right) and earlier Albatros aircraft, the LFG D.VI (above) had a load-carrying plywood skin. The fuselage of the LFG D.VI, however, was made of over-lapping strips of plywood ar-ranged like the hull planking of a small boat.

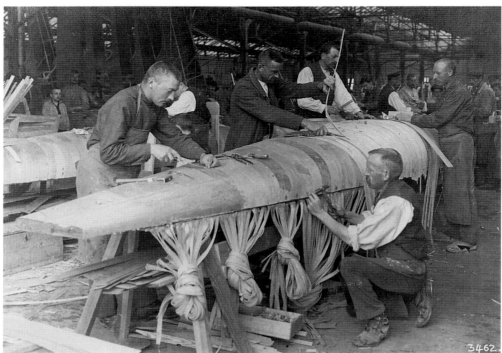

cantilever wing. This type of construction required no external bracing—all major supporting structures were contained within the wing itself. The cantilever wing was eventually incorporated into various Fokker aircraft as well.

Suitable lightweight alloys were not yet readily available in 1917, and so Hugo Junkers, designer of the Junkers J.I, stiffened inferior-quality aluminum by corrugating it. The corrugations did not increase the metal's strength, but made it stiffer along the length of each section.

Most of the new aircraft tested at Adlershof, however, used new combinations of traditional materials to achieve new heights in speed, maneuverability, and rate of climb. Spurred by shortages of raw materials, the German aircraft industry sought to maintain maximum production levels by developing alternative materials and construction methods. In addition to using wood to replace rubber tires and welded steel for the internal structure of fuselages, German manufacturers also found ways to use poor-quality wood that would normally have been discarded. By combining wood chips, scraps, and low-quality birch to produce plywood aircraft skinning, the German aircraft industry overcame shortages of high-quality woods.

The fuselage of the Pfalz D.XII, for example, had strips of plywood wrapped around its internal framework in a spiral fashion. This wooden skin construction added strength to the fuselage and allowed the Pfalz to have a simpler—and lighter—internal framework than fabric-skinned aircraft, which relied entirely on their framework for strength.

Cantilevered wings, stressed skin, and all-metal aircraft became hallmarks of postwar aircraft. During the last few months of the war, however, these technologically advanced airplanes played only a minor role. To support a final offensive on the Western Front in the spring of 1918, German military leaders committed all available aircraft, including aircraft tested at Adlershof, obsolete Albatroses, and innovative Fokker D.VIIs.

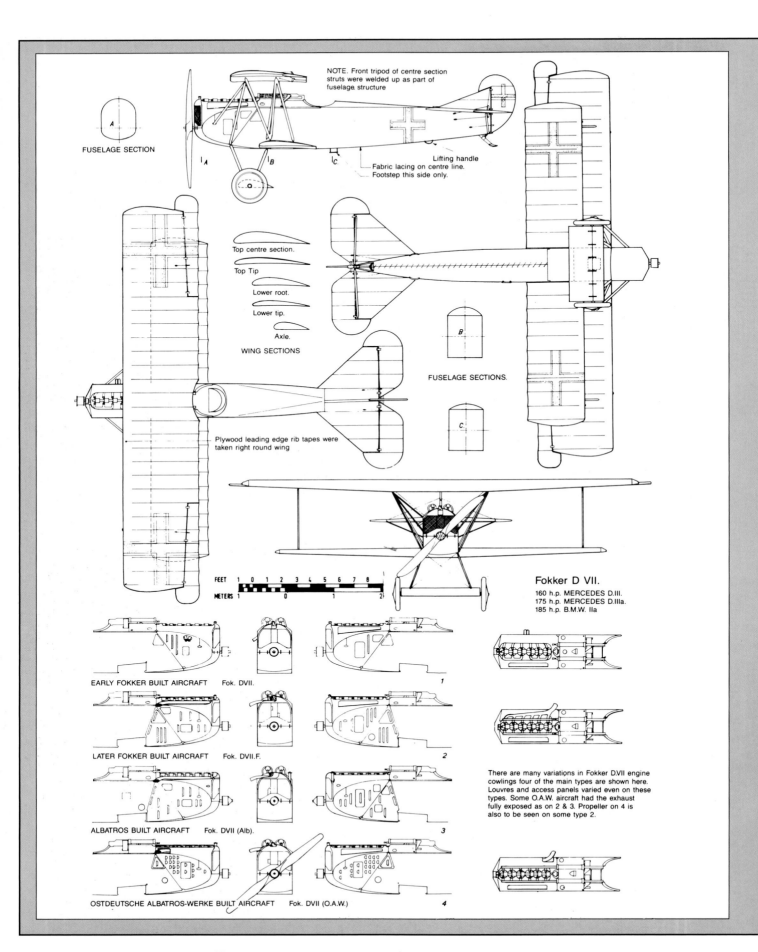

NOTE. Front tripod of centre section struts were welded up as part of fuselage structure

FUSELAGE SECTION

A

Lifting handle
Fabric lacing on centre line.
Footstep this side only.

Top centre section.

Top Tip

Lower root.

Lower tip.

Axle.

WING SECTIONS

Plywood leading edge rib tapes were taken right round wing

B

C

FUSELAGE SECTIONS.

FEET 1 0 1 2 3 4 5 6 7 8
METERS 1   0   1   2

Fokker D VII.
160 h.p. MERCEDES D.III.
175 h.p. MERCEDES D.IIIa.
185 h.p. B.M.W. IIa

EARLY FOKKER BUILT AIRCRAFT   Fok. DVII.   1

LATER FOKKER BUILT AIRCRAFT   Fok. DVII.F.   2

ALBATROS BUILT AIRCRAFT   Fok. DVII (Alb).   3

There are many variations in Fokker D.VII engine cowlings four of the main types are shown here. Louvres and access panels varied even on these types. Some O.A.W. aircraft had the exhaust fully exposed as on 2 & 3. Propeller on 4 is also to be seen on some type 2.

OSTDEUTSCHE ALBATROS-WERKE BUILT AIRCRAFT   Fok. DVII (O.A.W.)   4

The Fokker D.VII

Desperate to find a suitable replacement for the obsolete Albatros D.Va, but not ready to accept the most radical new aircraft designs, German military leaders selected the Fokker D.VII for mass production in April 1918.

The innovative design features that made the Fokker D.VII superior to the Albatros D.Va could be produced without resorting to new manufacturing processes. The Fokker D.VII's cantilever wing required few external bracing wires, thus accelerating the assembly process. Using welded steel tubing for the fuselage's internal framework prevented shortages of aircraft-quality wood from delaying production and provided the aircraft with a light and strong frame.

To maintain such an airplane as the Albatros D.Va, the Fokker D.VII's predecessor, ground crews constantly adjusted the airplane's (wire-bracing) rigging. Because the Fokker's wings were internally braced and had no external rigging, maintenance was simpler. With less time in the shop, the limited German fighter force could spend more time in combat.

The NASM's Fokker D.VII was manufactured by the Ostdeutsche Albatros Werke (East German Albatros Works) in 1918. Its pilot, Lt. Heinz von Beaulieu-Marconnay, had served with the 10th Uhlan (Cavalry) Regiment before becoming a pilot. To honor his old unit, von Beaulieu-Marconnay marked his fighter with the legend "U.10." The aircraft was captured on November 9, 1918, when its pilot mistakenly landed at an airfield occupied by the U.S. Army Air Service's 95th Squadron.

The Smithsonian acquired the aircraft in 1920 from the U.S. War Department. It was originally restored in 1970 and completely refurbished in 1990 for *Legend, Memory, and the Great War in the Air*.

The pilot of what would become the Smithsonian's Fokker D.VII mistakenly landed his aircraft on an American airfield in France only two days before the Armistice that ended the war took effect. The aircraft is seen here shortly after the end of the war, carrying the kicking mule insignia of the U.S. Army Air Service's 95th Squadron.

Because it was internally braced, the Fokker D.VII was easier to maintain than wood-and-fabric aircraft.

VI Strategic Bombing: A New Kind of Warfare

STRATEGIC BOMBING REMAINS one of the most controversial and far-reaching legacies of the first war in the air. The path to Hiroshima and the real possibility of nuclear holocaust began during World War I, when cities were bombed for the first time in history. Strategic bombing—using aircraft to attack an enemy's cities, industries, and civilian population—redefined the battlefield and erased forever the distinction between soldier and civilian. By the end of the war the bomber had emerged as one of the principal weapons of the twentieth century.

SOPWITH 7F.1 SNIPE

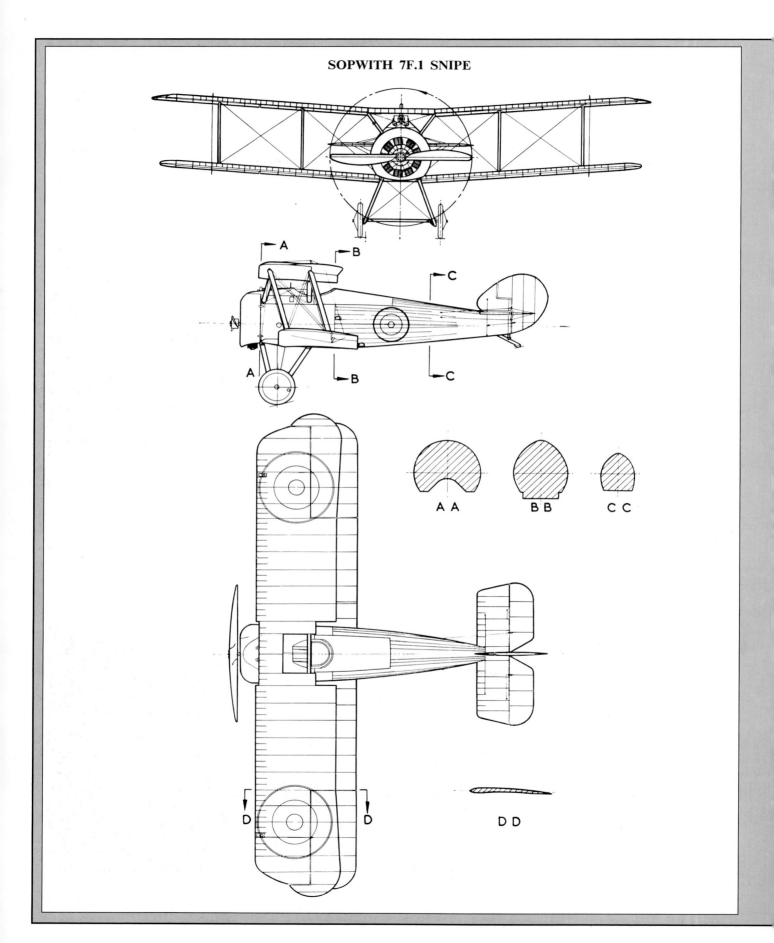

A A

B B

C C

D D

Sopwith 7F.1 Snipe:
The RAF's first standard fighter

At the outbreak of World War I, Britain had neither an independent air force nor a home defense force to guard against aerial attack. By the end of the war, it had both. Created in reaction to the German strategic bombing campaign against Britain, the Royal Air Force was intended to defend against further attacks and to bomb German cities in retaliation. To equip their home defense squadrons, the commanders of this first independent air force chose the Sopwith 7F.1 Snipe as their standard fighter in 1918.

Developed around the new and powerful Bentley BR-2 rotary engine, the Snipe began its career as a replacement for the Sopwith Camel fighter of 1917. This transition to the new fighter had barely begun when the war ended, but Snipes did equip three squadrons on the Western Front. After the war, as the standard fighter of the RAF, Snipes served in many home defense squadrons, some soldiering on until the late twenties.

Production versions of the Snipe had two sets of struts connecting the upper and lower wings, a stronger con-figuration than the prototype's single set. This arrangement increased drag, causing a decrease in top speed, so the Snipe offered no speed advantage over the Camel. The Snipe did retain the Camel's excellent maneuverability, but was considerably easier to control.

The Sopwith 7F.1 Snipe exhibited at the National Air and Space Museum is the only surviving example of its type. It was built as a two-seat trainer in 1918. After the war it was one of four Snipes purchased and brought to the United States by motion picture actor and pilot Reginald Denny. In 1928 the aircraft was purchased by Howard Hughes for his epic film *Hell's Angels*. It also appeared in both versions of *The Dawn Patrol*. After its movie career ended, the aircraft was purchased by Cole Palen for his Old Rhinebeck Aerodrome in New York. In 1989 the aircraft was lent to the National Air and Space Museum. It has been refurbished in the markings of No. 4 Squadron of the Royal Australian Flying Corps, one of the three squadrons that flew Snipes during the war.

An early production Snipe, photographed in Britain shortly after the end of the war.

For the first time in history, civilians found themselves under the threat of aerial attack. The inhabitants of London sought protection from air raids in the city's underground railway system. This German postcard of 1916 shows the hysterical reaction that Germany hoped its Zeppelin raids would provoke.

Strategic bombing had been foreseen even before sustained, controlled flight had been achieved. In *The War in the Air*, a 1908 novel that predicted the nature of future wars, author H. G. Wells described a devastating airship attack on New York. Wells's writings fed the popular belief that airships, with their enormous range and load-carrying abilities, would be used to attack enemy cities. Fear of attack by Zeppelins was widespread in London and Paris, which were in their range, and even extended to the United States, leading to false sightings of German airships over New York on several occasions.

Zeppelin Raids

> *Zeppelin, flieg,*
> *Hilf uns im Krieg*
> *Flieg nach England,*
> *England wird abgebrannt,*
> *Zeppelin, flieg!*

> *Zeppelin, fly,*
> *Help us in the war*
> *Fly to England,*
> *England shall be destroyed with fire,*
> *Zeppelin, fly!*

GERMAN CHILDREN'S SONG

Once the war began, moral, political, and technological factors initially prevented any of the belligerents from conducting attacks on civilian targets. By war's end, however, most of the belligerents had bombed enemy cities. Of these attacks, the German bombing of Britain, which lasted from 1915 to 1918, was the most extensive campaign of the war and had the most profound military and political effects.

Concerned about the potential repercussions of bombing cities and their inhabitants, Kaiser Wilhelm II at first overruled the requests of German army and navy airship commanders to bomb London. As the war on the Western Front became bogged down during the winter of 1915, the Kaiser, increasingly desperate to take Britain out of the war and unable to attack the British Isles by any other means, began to relax his restrictions against bombing British cities. German airship commanders were finally allowed to bomb targets in Britain during the first months of 1915, but were restricted from attacking cultural monuments, churches, or residential areas.

Londoners expected aerial attacks from the beginning of the war. Posters identifying various airplanes and airships helped spotters distinguish between friendly and enemy aircraft.

Capable of flying higher and farther with a larger bomb load than any airplane in 1914, Zeppelins seemed the most threatening type of bomber aircraft at the outbreak of hostilities. However, the airships were difficult to fly in high winds and vulnerable to incendiary bullets because they were filled with highly explosive hydrogen gas.

This rare photograph of the interior of a Zeppelin control gondola was taken aboard German Navy Zeppelin L-49, which was downed in France while returning from a night bombing raid against Britain on October 20, 1917. After high winds had blown the Zeppelin many miles off course, the L-49's commander, desperate to find a recognizable landmark, ordered the airship to descend. French fighters found and attacked the L-49, but lacked the incendiary ammunition necessary to ignite the Zeppelin. After losing much of its hydrogen gas through holes caused by the fighters' guns, the L-49 landed intact behind Allied lines.

The Germans hoped to destroy British cities by igniting them with incendiary bombs dropped from Zeppelins. But the bombs proved to be too small, too unreliable, and too easily extinguished.

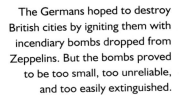

Designed without the benefit of wartime experience, bombs carried by the Zeppelins at the beginning of the war were not aerodynamically shaped, making accurate bombing impossible. These "bowling balls" were intended to damage buildings, which would then be ignited by incendiary bombs, but they proved highly unreliable. In contrast to the early Zeppelin bombs, the P.u.W. bomb (left) was aerodynamic in shape. Developed by the German Testing Section and Air Service Workshops (*Prüfanstalt und Werft der Fliegertruppen*), the P.u.W. bomb had three angled fins to spin the bomb as it descended, which improved targeting accuracy. The shift to night bombing in September 1917 made this improvement largely irrelevant. Because darkness obscured the targets, accurate bombing was impossible.

The British recognized that a Zeppelin's hydrogen-filled envelope was extremely vulnerable to incendiary (explosive) bullets. Because of difficulties in developing bullets that would not ignite prematurely, British pilots had to rely on such weapons as the Rankin dart on the left. Rather than being fired from a gun, the Rankin dart was to be dropped on an airship from above, piercing the airship's gas bags, and igniting the hydrogen inside. Although the dart seemed a good alternative to explosive bullets, British fighters rarely proved capable of flying high enough to allow an attack to be made on a Zeppelin from above. The failure of the Rankin dart convinced British military leaders to speed up development and production of incendiary ammunition. Buckingham machine-gun ammunition on the right incorporated a bullet that contained phosphorus, which ignited on contact with air. Because it was easier to hit an airship with machine-gun fire, the incendiary bullet was more effective than bombs or Rankin darts. Its development had been so accelerated that the ammunition was rife with defects. The phosphorus filling of the bullet was sometimes unstable and exploded prematurely, with disastrous results for the pilot.

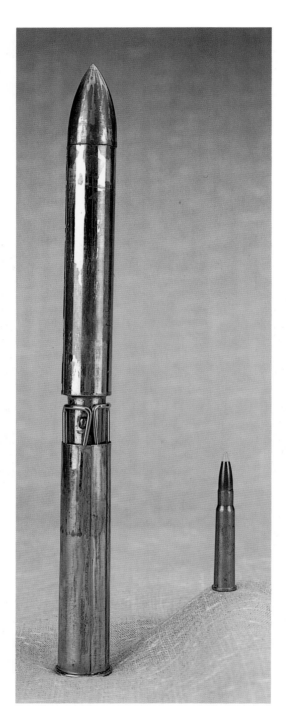

Experience soon showed that such restrictions were simply not practicable. Zeppelin crews, who often had difficulty finding the London metropolitan area at all, were unable to bomb targets in the city without killing civilians. As a result, the Kaiser gradually eased his earlier restrictions and permitted his airships to bomb British cities without regard to civilian casualties. For the next three years, Germany waged the first strategic bombing campaign against a civilian population. Although German airship and, later, bomber crews officially sought to attack military targets, undermining the morale of the British population increasingly became the campaign's primary objective.

Despite the great confidence of the airship commanders, the Zeppelin raids never managed to inflict any more than minor damage. Vulnerable to bad weather and to incendiary bullets from enemy fighters, the German airships proved as dangerous to their crews as to British civilians. Although bombs dropped from Zeppelins killed 556 people in Britain and injured another 1,358, the raiders themselves suffered severe losses. From the first major raid in May 1915 to the last in October 1918, seventeen airships were destroyed, their crews of ten or more often incinerated with them.

Gothas Attack London by Day

By the end of 1916, mounting losses of Zeppelins to antiaircraft artillery fire and British aircraft convinced Germany to seek alternative means of bombing Britain. The G-Class or *Grosskampfflugzeug* (large battle airplane) seemed to be the answer. Although a single G-Class bomber could not carry as many bombs as an airship, its speed made interception by British fighters much more difficult.

Expecting the bombers to cause great physical and psychological damage, the *Luftstreitkräfte* (Imperial German Air Service) planned a concerted bomber offensive against Britain for 1917. Rather than flying at night as the Zeppelins had done, German G-Class aircraft, such as the Gotha, Friedrichshafen, and A.E.G. bombers, executed a series of daring daylight raids on London and other targets in the British Isles from June to September 1917.

The first raid on London seemed to justify the high hopes of German planners for the bombing campaign. Encountering little opposition from British defenses, which were organized

and equipped to intercept airships at night, German bombers reached London from bases in Belgium late on the morning of June thirteenth, methodically circled in formation over the city's astonished inhabitants, dropped their bombs, and returned to base without loss. A second daylight raid on the British capital on July seventh produced similar results, but the shock of the attacks had motivated the British to improve their defenses. German losses increased as a result, and after another three daylight raids, the final nineteen raids on Britain were flown under the cover of darkness.

Although the bombs dropped by the German bombers over the course of more than twenty attacks caused relatively few casualties (857 killed and 2,051 injured) and failed to measurably affect Britain's ability to wage war, the raids nonetheless had enormous consequences.

British Response

After the second German daylight air raid on London, British civilians demanded better defenses and retaliation against German cities. Responding to the public uproar, the British War Cabinet formed the Prime Minister's Committee on Air Organization and Home Defense against Air Raids. The committee was established to evaluate Britain's air services and home defense organization and to recommend improvements.

Concerned about civil unrest and possible loss of war production caused by workers leaving their jobs during air raids, the committee recommended the formation of the London Air Defense Area to coordinate the aerial defense of southeastern England, the formation of additional home defense fighter squadrons, and, most importantly, the creation of an independent air force. These recommendations indicate to some

These Gotha bombers on an airfield near Gontrode, Belgium, are among those that raided London during 1917.

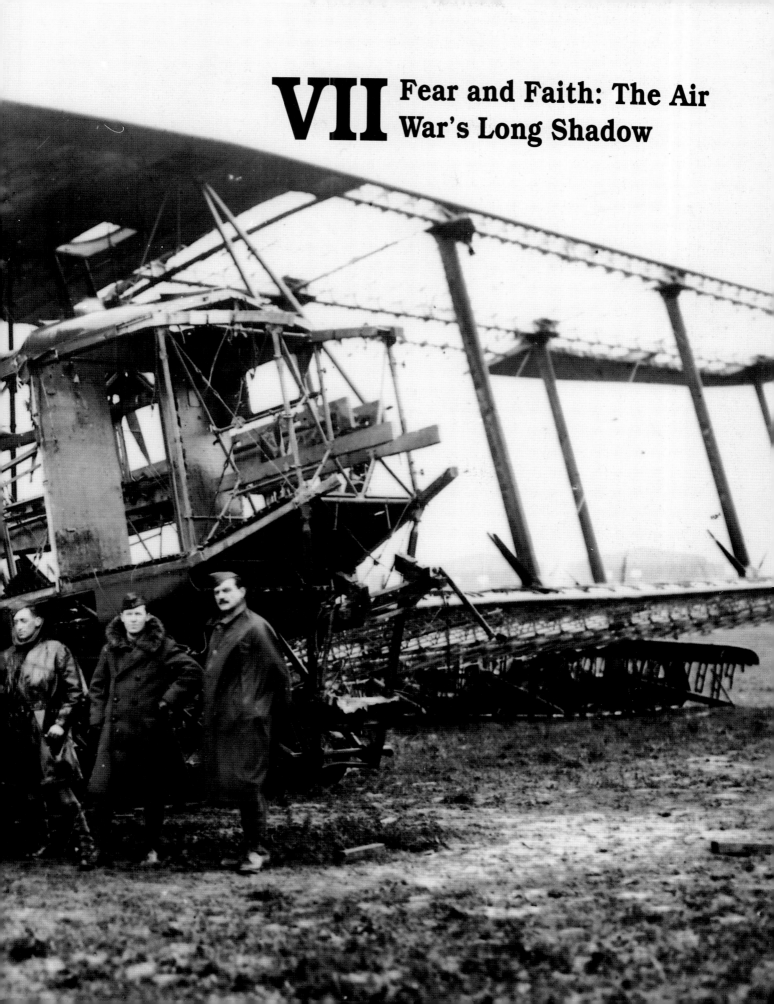

VII Fear and Faith: The Air War's Long Shadow

The Treaty of Versailles, which ended the war with Germany, was one of the first serious, if one-sided, attempts to restrict the bomber. The agreement reached during the Paris Peace Conference of 1919 forbade Germany from possessing an air force.

RIGHT:

Air power advocates, including American General William "Billy" Mitchell, sought to convince their governments that the bomber represented the best means to avoid another costly global war.

PREVIOUS PAGE:

The terms of the Armistice that ended the war required Germany to surrender its military aircraft, especially "all night bombers," to the victorious Allies. By 1919 German airfields were littered with abandoned military aircraft, including some of the Zeppelin-Staaken bombers that had raided London the year before.

BY WAR'S END IN NOVEMBER 1918, more than 11 million people had died, revolutions had toppled governments in Russia and Germany, and the United States had risen to the first rank of the world's powers. The war changed the world's social and political order, but the Armistice that ended it ultimately helped bring about a second, even more devastating world war only twenty-one years later.

Although the airplane did not prove to be a decisive weapon, it clearly demonstrated its potential. Reacting to the political outcry that followed aerial attacks on their cities, the authors of the Treaty of Versailles included a provision that forbade Germany from possessing an air force. Despite these measures, the memory of the terror caused by bombing raids against civilians lingered long after the guns had fallen silent. This and other lessons of the air war—however misinterpreted and distorted they might seem in retrospect—have shaped strategic planning since the war and changed the nature of warfare forever.

The Cult of Air Power

During the years immediately following the war, a vocal group of aviation advocates asserted that strategic bombing represented the only way to avoid another costly global war. Drawing on their wartime experiences, these prophets of air power—Guilio Douhet, William "Billy" Mitchell, and Sir Hugh Trenchard—presented their ideas in books, memoranda, and magazine articles and pressed their governments to create and maintain independent air forces equipped primarily with bombers. By 1939 their theories had created a cult of air power, formed the basis for the strategic bombing doctrine embraced by the United States and Britain, and spurred the development of the aircraft used for the extraordinarily destructive bombing campaigns of World War II.

Italian air power advocate Guilio Douhet had begun writing about military aviation before World War I. After briefly commanding the Italian Army's aviation battalion at the beginning of the war, Douhet spent over a year in prison, partly as a result of a prewar article he had written predicting military disaster for Italy. Released in 1918, he again briefly commanded the Italian air service during the final months of the war.

Adolf Hitler's rise to power brought an end to any serious attempt to limit the bomber and spurred France and Britain to begin their own bomber development programs. The Nazis' creation of a bomber-equipped air force, in violation of the Treaty of Versailles, was a significant step toward World War II.

Aerial attacks on cities during the Spanish Civil War provided the first evidence since World War I of what bombing could do to urban areas and how the inhabitants of a targeted town would react. These Stukas of the German Condor Legion were used for attacks on a number of Loyalist-held cities during 1939.

The Legacies of World War I in the Air

The heroic image of the fighter pilot—as depicted by such movies as *Top Gun*—remains popular today, little changed from the image of the World War I fighter ace. Although the performance and complexity of the aircraft he flies far exceeds that of the aircraft of the Great War, the fighter pilot remains a reassuring symbol of human control of technology.

In contrast to the romantic image of the military aviator, uncertainty about mankind's ability to control military aviation's destructiveness is an equally persistent legacy of World War I. From biplanes to ICBMs, the debate over the effectiveness and morality of aerial weapons has remained unresolved.

Movie poster for
The Dawn Patrol, 1930

Movie poster for
Top Gun, 1986.

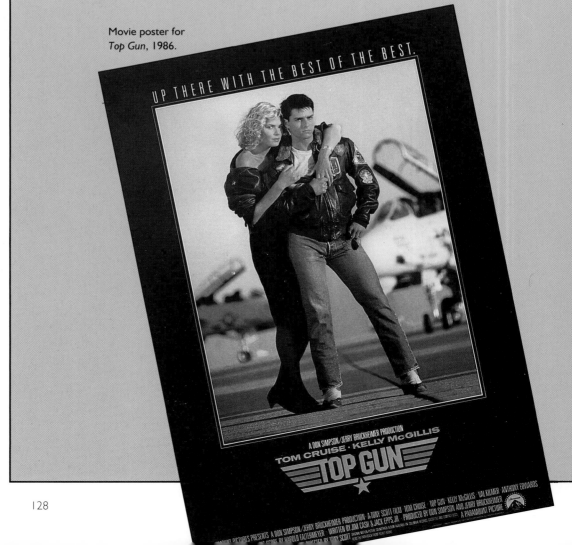

Disarmament poster, 1919.

Disarmament poster, circa 1972.

The bombing doctrine of the U.S. Army Air Forces on the eve of World War II called for precision daylight bombing of enemy industry. Operational realities, however, spurred air force planners to begin area bombing in October 1943. By the summer of 1944 U.S. bombers, such as these B-17s of the Eighth Air Force, operated more freely over Germany but continued to bomb urban areas when clouds obscured industrial targets.

Despite his limited experience with military aviation, by 1918 Douhet was deeply impressed with the effects of the war's limited strategic bombing campaigns. Believing that World War I had demonstrated the indecisiveness of armies and navies, Douhet asserted that only aircraft could decide future wars by flying over the battlefield to bomb enemy cities. Societies under the stress of total war, he argued, would quickly collapse when subjected to aerial bombardment. More prophet than theorist, Douhet made his most strident appeal for air power in 1921 in *Il dominio dell'aria* (*The Command of the Air*), a book that exaggerated the bomber's destructive capabilities and underestimated the ability of civilians to withstand aerial attack.

In the political atmosphere of Fascist Italy, Douhet's theories, including his arguments for aerial attacks on cities and the use of incendiary and poison gas bombs, received widespread attention. By the end of the 1930s, Italy possessed one of the largest air forces in the world, due in no small measure to Douhet's promotion of military aviation. Although

his writings were not widely translated and distributed before the 1930s, Douhet's theories and predictions about the destructiveness of the next air war nevertheless influenced the thinking of air power advocates and opponents alike during the interwar years.

In Britain, Chief of Air Staff Sir Hugh Trenchard struggled to justify the continuing existence of an independent air force by using squadrons of the greatly reduced Royal Air Force to quell unrest in remote areas of the British Empire. These "Air Control" operations, which included bombing Iraqi, Indian, and Afghan villages suspected of harboring guerrillas, probably saved the Royal Air Force, but provided little information about how European civilians would react to attacks on their own cities.

Although Trenchard considered the reduction of civilian morale to be a legitimate goal of strategic bombing, he believed that indiscriminate bombing of cities was unacceptable. In a 1928 memorandum, however, Trenchard asserted that "incidental destruction of civilian life

The Allied strategic bombing campaigns were extraordinarily destructive, razing most of the major cities in Germany and Japan and killing at least a million civilians. The efficacy of the bombing in hastening enemy surrender is debated to this day.

and property" as a result of attacks on military targets situated in cities should not deter the bombing of "centers of production, transportation and communication."

The RAF leaders who followed Trenchard during the 1930s did little to clarify policy with respect to the bombing of civilians. The outbreak of World War II finally forced the RAF to formulate and execute a strategy for bombing Germany. The large-scale bombing campaign that began in 1942 cost the lives of over 58,000 airmen and killed more than 500,000 people on the ground, but it failed to bring about a collapse of either the German war economy or civilian morale.

In the United States, where the experience of America's first military intervention in Europe had led to disillusionment with foreign entanglements and to isolationism, the U.S. Army Air Service was quickly pared down after the war. Fearing the possible disestablishment of the air service, Gen. William "Billy" Mitchell attempted to generate support for his theories by conducting controversial bombing demonstrations against

decommissioned or captured warships off the Virginia Capes during 1921. Among the vessels selected for the tests was the ex-Imperial German Navy battleship *Ostfriesland*, which was purported to be unsinkable.

The unmanned, undefended battleships, whose watertight integrity was compromised by open hatches, quickly sank after being hit with numerous bombs, some of which were far larger than the limit agreed to by Mitchell before the exercise. Mitchell exaggerated the significance of the tests, asserting that they had clearly demonstrated the effectiveness of air power, the obsolescence of surface navies, and the need for an independent air force.

Ignoring official skepticism and military regulations, Mitchell became an increasingly strident crusader for air power. In 1925 he completed *Winged Defense*, a book in which he presented his air power theories and argued for an air force separate from the army and navy. By 1926 his superiors had had enough, and Mitchell was court-martialed for insubordination. Mitchell's

Thermonuclear explosion, 1952. The advent
of the nuclear age in 1945 represented strategic bombing's maturation, but also created
an unresolved dilemma. Today, more than
75 years after the first bombing of civilians,
we continue to live under the long shadow
of strategic bombing.

army career was over, but his disciples, who shared his faith in the bomber and viewed him as a martyr to the cult of air power, continued to develop his theories and lobbied for an air force separate from the army and navy.

Working in relative obscurity, Mitchell's disciples at the Air Corps Tactical School (ACTS) first developed American strategic bombing doctrine. Initially, the Army Air Corps' policy included attacks on civilian targets. By the mid-1930s new technology, such as the Norden bombsight, promised the capability of attacking enemy industry accurately but without high civilian casualties. Air Corps leaders justified funding for the bomber intended to conduct such attacks by alleging the need for a coastal *defense* aircraft. Considering the isolationist sentiment of the 1930s, it is unlikely that the public would have supported a long-range bomber like the Boeing B-17 Flying Fortress for any purpose other than the *defense* of the United States.

Fear of the Bomber

While the air power prophets asserted that an independent air force equipped with bombers would be the only effective deterrent against enemy aerial attacks, others addressed the threat of aerial attack by seeking to ban the bomber altogether. Legal experts from the United States, Great Britain, France, Italy, Japan, and the Netherlands met in the Hague from December 1922 to February 1923 to develop limitations on aerial bombing under a framework of international law. Although the jurists did not attempt to limit the number of bombers in each country's air service, the Hague Draft Rules they composed were intended to provide the legal basis for limiting bombing in future wars. The rules prohibited terror bombing of civilians, but allowed attacks on military targets, thereby providing a loophole that rendered meaningless the prohibition on the bombing of civilians.

Even with such flaws, the code drafted at the Hague was an international attempt to recognize and limit the destructive potential of the bomber. Because many of the participants at the conference feared losing the ability to retaliate against enemy bombing, the Hague Draft Rules were never ratified, and were therefore not legally binding. Nevertheless, most of the participants, including the United States and Britain, observed the rules voluntarily until World War II.

The second and final conference to limit

the bomber began in Geneva during February 1932. In addition to the nations that had attended the earlier conference at the Hague, the Geneva Disarmament Conference included representatives from the Soviet Union and Germany. Although a number of the participants, including Britain, France, and the United States, seemed willing to negotiate significant restrictions on the size of bomber forces, Adolf Hitler's rise to power in January 1933 scuttled any chance that the conference might have had for success. After withdrawing from the talks and then from the League of Nations in October, the Nazi government began the accelerated rearming of the German military, including the construction of an independent air force equipped with bombers. Reacting to the predictions of the air power theorists and the fears of their civilian populations, Britain and France began their own programs of rearmament, which included the development and construction of fleets of bombers that, it was hoped, would deter German bombing.

The Long Shadow

The first bombing of cities, which had taken place during World War I, provided interwar air power advocates with the only hard evidence before 1937 about what such attacks could do. Advocates and opponents of air power could only speculate about the nature of the next air war. A few were optimistic: for instance, British Air Ministry official John Spaight theorized that the chivalrous nature of the aviator, which he felt was demonstrated during World War I, would prevent any bombing of civilians in future wars. Others believed that strategic bombing would lead to the end of European civilization.

The experience of the Spanish Civil War (1937–39) and the Sino-Japanese War (1937–45) provided the first evidence since World War I about the nature of strategic bombing and how civilians would react to the attacks. The evidence, however, was conflicting. Although the bombing of such Spanish cities as Barcelona and Guernica caused enormous destruction and undoubtedly contributed to the eventual Fascist victory in the Spanish Civil War, the attacks seemed to harden, rather lessen the will of the civilian population to resist. Similarly, although the air forces of Japan began bombing Chinese cities at the outbreak of the Sino-Japanese War in 1937, by 1941 Japan had been drawn into a quagmire on the Asian mainland from which neither its air nor ground forces could extricate themselves.